T0265785

THE
STORY
EDGE

THE
STORY
EDGE

How Leaders Harness the Power
of Stories to Win in Business

KINDRA HALL

HARPERCOLLINS
LEADERSHIP

AN IMPRINT OF HARPERCOLLINS

© 2024 Kindra Hall

Names and identifying characteristics of some individuals have been changed to preserve their privacy.

Published by HarperCollins Leadership, an imprint of HarperCollins Focus LLC.

Any internet addresses, phone numbers, or company or product information printed in this book are offered as a resource and are not intended in any way to be or to imply an endorsement by HarperCollins Leadership, nor does HarperCollins Leadership vouch for the existence, content, or services of these sites, phone numbers, companies, or products beyond the life of this book.

ISBN 978-1-4002-2861-4 (eBook)
ISBN 978-1-4002-2857-7 (HC)

Library of Congress Cataloging-in-Publication Data
Library of Congress Cataloging-in-Publication application has been submitted.

Printed in the United States of America
24 25 26 27 28 LBC 5 4 3 2 1

CONTENTS

INTRODUCTION

Our Evolutionary Edge . . . . *ix*

CHAPTER ONE

Manias and Truths *1*

CHAPTER TWO

But First, Story 19

There Is Always a Story

CHAPTER THREE

Know There's *Always* a Story
(. . . and You Can Save the World!) 35

CHAPTER FOUR

More Stories = Better Decisions 45

CHAPTER FIVE

Empathy 101 63

A Story Needs to Be Told

CHAPTER SIX
If You Want Something Done . . .
a Story Must Be Told 85

CHAPTER SEVEN
The Ultimate Influence Equation 103

CHAPTER EIGHT
Operation Inspiration 125

You're Always in the Middle of the Story

CHAPTER NINE
Smack Dab in the Middle 145

CHAPTER TEN
Optimism . . . Brought to You by Storytelling 159

CHAPTER ELEVEN
A Roadmap for Resilience 179

CONCLUSION
The Infinity Edge 197

CONTENTS

APPENDIX
The Story of Rocky the Raccoon 203

ACKNOWLEDGMENTS 205

NOTES 207

INDEX 217

ABOUT THE AUTHOR 225

Our Evolutionary Edge

We are storytellers.

Humans are here, today, because we can communicate through story.

Humans are here because we can *understand* a story.

Human evolution—be it the 400,000 years behind us or however many years we have ahead of us—is the result of our ability to connect, organize, and adapt both through the stories we tell and the stories we seek.

"What was the Sapiens' secret of success? How did we manage to settle so rapidly in so many distant and ecologically different habitats? How did we push all other human species into oblivion?"[1] Yuval Noah Harari asked in his 2015 book *Sapiens*.

And then he answered: "The most likely answer is the very thing that makes the debate possible: *Homo sapiens* conquered the world thanks above all to its unique language."[2]

What was unique about our language?

You guessed it. We could tell stories.

In fact, storytelling was so central to *Homo sapiens'* evolution that some have suggested a better name for our species is *Pan narrans*, or "the storytelling ape."[3]

Large-scale human cooperation was made possible by our ability to talk not only about the things that existed, but also about the concepts we couldn't see. Through stories, humans were able to communicate about the bison they ate and the lions they ran from, and also about who could be trusted and who was a liar. In doing so, stories give humans "the unprecedented ability to cooperate flexibly in large numbers."[4]

The impact of this, our storytelling nature, was the equivalent of the modern-day "cheat code." Evolution that would have otherwise required waiting tens of thousands of years for a genetic mutation, we were able to bypass completely. We skipped ahead. Storytelling was the big ladder in *Chutes and Ladders* or the FastPass at Disney— the thing that allowed us to cut the line and leave everyone else staring in envy.

As *Sapiens'* author Harari put it, because human cooperation is built on stories, by changing the story we told, we could revise behavior "rapidly in accordance with changing needs . . . This opened a fast lane of cultural evolution, bypassing the traffic jams of genetic evolution."[5]

Take the Catholic Church, for example, where the top leaders, the proverbial "alpha males," the popes and priests, take a vow of celibacy. A vow *not* to procreate. A vow that, if you were to suggest that to a lion or a gorilla or a beetle or a rabbit or *any other living creature on this planet*, their heads might explode. It is a vow that breaks one of the most fundamental laws of evolution. The thing that is a fundamental requirement of the continuation of a species. And yet the Catholic Church has survived generations of celibate male leadership. This survival occurred "not by passing on the 'celibacy gene' from one pope to the next, but by passing on the stories of the New Testament and of Catholic canon law."[6]

Life as we know it is possible because of our stories. It has been our evolutionary advantage since the beginning of time and yet . . . within our storied design, or perhaps *because* of it, lies a fundamental weakness.

We don't use our edge.

We ignore it.

Or forget to use it.

Or overtly underestimate it with flawed thinking like:

"There isn't enough *time* for a story" or "No one wants a story, they just want the facts."

What other animal would *ever* behave in this way?!

The scorpion doesn't ignore the fact that it has a tail full of venom and instead opt for a different survival mechanism when faced with a crisis. Bald eagles don't spend time pondering that their white feathers help camouflage them against the clouds when they hunt. Polar bears don't ruminate about how they evolved from omnivorous, dull-toothed brown grizzlies into white, sharp-toothed creatures to survive in harsh, arctic environments and hunt for seals rather than blueberries.

Other animals don't ignore or question the evolutionary edge they've been given.

Animals *lean into* natural selection and *optimize* their evolutionary advantage.

And it's time you did too.

This book is here to fix the ridiculous thinking that undervalues the very thing that makes business possible in the first place. To not only *remind* you of the power you have within you, but to offer simple solutions and strategies for *harnessing* the power of stories so that you can reclaim your evolutionary edge; because now more than ever, we need it if we want to survive the next phase of modernization.

And not just our ability to *tell* stories . . .

Excellence in managing the inevitable chaos that is ahead will require what I call **Story Forward leadership.** This is a holistic approach to innovation, connection, and problem-solving in business. It's an understanding that behind *every* problem and *every* person, there is a story. Story Forward leadership involves a mastery of telling stories to unite and include and build *belief* in something. It's developing an ability to—even amid the chaos—recognize that someday this, too, will be a story that can be told to teach, guide, and inspire others.

Regardless of what is ahead, storytelling remains the ultimate human advantage.

It is the original algorithm. The first currency.

Stories will continue to be our ultimate edge, just as they always have been.

On the pages that follow, I offer leaders a different approach to the future of work. We'll explore this evolutionary advantage more deeply. I'll explain how every problem you face is, indeed, a "story problem." You'll learn the three Truths of Story Forward leadership:

1. There is always a story,

2. A story needs to be told, and

3. You're always in the *middle* of a story (one that is being written right now).

I'll introduce you to fundamental phrases that will elevate any individual who puts them on repeat in their daily encounters. We'll discuss the business buzzwords that are haunting brand and executive boards right now, words such as "empathy," "authenticity," "transparency," "resilience," "belonging," "creativity," and "innovation." You will see how the Story Forward approach is the fastest path to achieving them all.

It is time to get back to the most important tool at our disposal—the *original* human edge: storytelling.

ONE

Manias and Truths

✕

"In the midst of movement and chaos,
keep stillness inside of you."
—DEEPAK CHOPRA

The place, Holland.

The time, somewhere in the early to mid-1600s.

The situation, complete mayhem.

A very wealthy man had been robbed of his most prized posses-
sion, and the house was being torn apart while everyone searched
for it.

Before the chaos broke out, the day began with some good news
for the wealthy man. A delivery had arrived, filled with assorted,
valuable merchandise—silks, velvets, goblets—and the rich man was
thrilled. So thrilled in fact, he insisted on giving the man who
brought the delivery, a sailor who had traveled a great distance, a fine
red herring to enjoy for breakfast. As the rich man went to collect
the herring from the kitchen, the sailor noticed a strange-looking
onion sitting among the treasures he had just delivered.

Whether because he was embarrassed that an unsightly vegetable had nestled itself among the riches, or because he really liked onions, or both, the sailor quickly grabbed the odd onion and put it in his pocket just as the rich man came back with the herring. The men exchanged gratitudes and the sailor returned to the dock. There he sat on a large, coiled rope and enjoyed the herring with a little onion relish as a bonus.

Imagine the sailor's surprise when, as he was finishing his final bite, he saw the rich man and what appeared to be an entire army of officers charging toward him.

"You ate my tulip!" the rich man hollered, his face red and bulging. The rich man pointed to the sailor, who was arrested on the spot, with a bit of onion still sitting delicately upon his lip.

Except, it wasn't an onion.

It was a tulip bulb.

A *Semper Augustus* bulb.

The most valuable item among those the rich man had received that day.

A tulip bulb worth enough to *lavishly* feed an entire *crew* of sailors . . . for a *year*.[1]

IT'S TRUE. Long before cryptocurrency, NFTs, or Lamborghinis, there were tulip bulbs. The rarest of the bulbs were traded for as much as six times the average annual salary. Some bulbs, in today's equivalent currency, cost as much as a million dollars each. A single bulb was considered an acceptable dowry for a bride. People mortgaged their homes to buy them, either to signal their wealth or in hopes of selling them at a profit.[2]

If you have read about this "Tulipmania" (also known as the "Tulip Craze"), chances are it was in an economics class. It's cited as the classic example of a financial bubble where the price of something rapidly escalates, not because its true value increases, but due to (greedy and speculative) market behavior.

Because, as your econ professor likely told you: bubbles burst. When, in England and Holland, the tulip market crashed way back in 1637, many families lost their fortunes and were left destitute. It also makes sense why visiting the Netherlands during tulip season is a bucket list–worthy endeavor—the tulips are, so I've heard, spectacular.

It sounds a little absurd looking back, doesn't it? *Tulips?* That tulip bulbs could create such madness, such mania? Maybe . . . but it was also very serious. Just ask the sailor who accidentally ate the million-dollar almost-flower and was charged with a felony and thrown in prison for months.

Though tulips are not our current vice, that doesn't mean we are too evolved to fall victim to modern manias—remember Beanie Babies? Or the mania to join Clubhouse? Some manias are widespread while others are industry specific. Whatever the mania, when it comes to leadership, getting caught up in it is never a good look.

Gary Burnison, CEO of Korn Ferry, a global organizational consulting firm specializing in talent acquisition, leadership development, and organization strategy for Fortune 100 companies, warned against this tendency: "It's so easy these days to become entrenched in our environment, letting the moment direct our leadership style."[3]

The word *moment* is key.

While there is something to say for seizing the moment, moments are also fleeting. They are known to change from one to the next.

Allowing moments, with all their innate frivolity, to dictate the way you lead and work is dangerous.

There are manias born of the moment; and there are Truths.

There are things that evolve and are created because of the human nature to pursue and improve . . . and then there are things that never change. Things that are the constant, the baseline, the denominator, the control. These Truths make everything else possible, and the ability to differentiate between the two—a mania of the moment and a fundamental, unwavering truth—is a skill leaders in the modern world of work cannot afford to live without.

For practice, let's take a closer look at three (though there were many) of the big manias of 2023—Artificial Intelligence, Automation-Everything, and Rapid Change or Else.

THE ARTIFICIAL INTELLIGENCE
MANIA VS. THE AI TRUTH

For a while there was a trend on social media in which people admitted to (and even celebrated) their quirky flaws and unusual bad habits, declaring them "toxic traits." These lighthearted posts included admissions of things like preferring a spoon to eat a meal when most people would use a fork, and using retail therapy to deal with everyday frustrations. Some people revealed secretly liking pop songs they were supposed to hate. At least one person revealed their deep desire to domesticate a raccoon . . . you get the idea.

If you're like me, perhaps you have also considered what your "toxic trait" might be. And while I certainly have many, one stands out: I believe I will someday get through the newspapers that have piled up in various corners of my home.

Every day, the *Wall Street Journal* arrives on my doorstep and, every weekend day, the *New York Times*. Do I read these papers daily? No. Is anyone in my house allowed to dispose of a newspaper before I've read it? *Absolutely not.* I simply cannot bear the thought of missing a story. Even if they're obsolete or irrelevant, it *pains* me to think of a paper discarded, the stories unread. This means entire pieces of furniture are fully overtaken by stacks of newspapers, and I routinely read about events going on in the world six months after they've occurred.

Several years ago, this would have meant I was just a little behind when chatting with friends or colleagues about current events. Now, reading the paper from a few months before, or even a few weeks . . . let's face it, even just *days*, the old headlines read like punch lines.

More important, because of my toxic trait of collecting newspapers but not reading them until months later, I was one of the last people to learn of ChatGPT, the AI software that, based on a quick search of the NYT website, was first mentioned in the *Times* on December 5, 2022.

There, technology columnist Kevin Roose described ChatGPT as "quite simply, the best artificial intelligence chatbot ever released to the general public."[4] The interface was mentioned almost daily and then multiple times a day in the coming weeks and months in the newspapers that were piled up around my house, unread and untouched.

I was blissfully unaware of ChatGPT until one afternoon I was talking to a colleague and fellow writer whose mood seemed uncharacteristically foul during a discussion regarding chapter outlines and the writing process.

As if out of the blue, he stopped mid-sentence and said, "Things are changing. I think within the next five years, ChatGPT could write every single one of the books I've written . . ."

What? How could that be possible?

Perhaps it was because of my flippant attitude that my friend promptly asked the AI interface, to which he had acquired early access, to "write me a story about a raccoon who wanted to be human." Like a good little robot, ChatGPT did as it was told.

If you want to read the unedited, 389-word story about a raccoon (whom ChatGPT named "Rocky"), you can find it in its entirety in the back of this book. Suffice it to say, at first glance the story is not terrible. It has some *Animal Farm* + *Little Mermaid* "Part of Your World" vibes. It even ends with a cute little affirming adage: "We are all unique and special in our own way."

Now, if you were a fourth grader and had an assignment due for class in an hour and were required to write a 350-word story about a raccoon who wanted to be a human, this would likely do the trick. However, I'm doubtful acing fourth-grade writing assignments is high on your list of priorities right now.

THE ARTIFICIAL INTELLIGENCE TRUTH IS...

I was at a local women's event in New York City and was chatting with a woman who worked, *in AI development,* for a large, well-known, at the "forefront of the AI revolution" company and, of course, ChatGPT came up in conversation. "I'm just so surprised that everyone is getting so worked up about this all of a sudden. I've been personally working on this technology, it's been in practice, used, every day . . . for *ten years!* Why are people going so crazy about it *now?*" It was not the response I was expecting—certainly the only time someone had talked about AI without stars in their eyes and a hint of overwhelm (good or bad) in their voice.

That's when I knew, we were wrapped up in a mania.

The *truth* is, artificial intelligence requires *human* intelligence. *We* are the input. *We* are the model. Certainly it can be used as a powerful tool—but when it comes to creativity, inspiration, true connection, AI can only draw from what humans have already created. Are there legitimate things to be concerned about? Definitely. With the rapid advancement of artificial technology come new threats and dangers to be considered. Will AI really cause the end of the world? Will it unlock a whole new level of life as we know it? Only time will tell. Regardless, reflecting on the similarities between AI and Tulipmania will serve a leader well.

THE AUTOMATION-EVERYTHING MANIA VS. THE AUTOMATION TRUTH

On June 13, 2023, the *Wall Street Journal* published an article entitled "Welcome to White Castle. Would You Like Human Interaction With That?" about an AI–enabled chatbot named Julia, who was now taking orders at the drive-thru window at a White Castle fast-food location.

While the restaurant executives praised her efficiency, customers were still unsure. Their reactions ranged from "freaked out" to calling the experience "a pain in the butt." Having to ask multiple times for an order of onion rings because the robot didn't understand the request and repeatedly shouting their acceptance of the terms and conditions of ordering from a robot were definite turnoffs. Three out of ten customers demanded to speak to a human—a human who was monitoring every interaction should Julia need assistance.

(For all the talk of streamlining, I can't help asking: When has redundancy ever equaled efficiency?)

While the threat of being replaced by robots began decades ago (I blame Rosie from *The Jetsons*), it's recently reached a new fever pitch. Just over one year prior to publication of this book, *Business Insider* released, and then continued to update, a list of the top ten jobs most likely at risk as a result of technology.[5] Those in the legal field, computer programming, media and advertising, and market research analysis were a few with a big red X.

Make no mistake, some automation is inevitable and already happening. Like when, in November 2022, after sixty-six years and with some people employed for twenty-five, even thirty-five years, New York toll booths were officially closed and the system fully automated. Or that you can now shop in a clothing store, throw your chosen garments in a bin at the checkout, and somehow the exact items are magically scanned, a total is magically (and accurately) generated, and you are just one credit card tap away from walking out of the store with almost zero human interaction at the point-of-sale, feeling like you stole something.

However, believing that automation technology is the ultimate panacea is only fueling the problems—like a lack of connection, the drought of motivation—that are holding businesses back. Fewer humans and less interaction does *not* necessarily equal better business.

THE AUTOMATION-EVERYTHING TRUTH IS . . .

Humans need humans.

For a myriad of reasons.

One, because often, a human is simply better at the job. Like when your flight gets canceled. Sure, if you only *kind of* want to get where you're going, you can use the app or automated voice tree. But if you *actually* want to get where you're trying to go, yelling "representative!" repeatedly into the phone to get a human on the line is usually the only way to make it happen.

Second, yes. People can be annoying. Avoiding them can feel like the solution. However, we are wired for sociability. "We are uniquely equipped with a neural and biochemical reward system that leaves us subjectively happier and objectively healthier after connecting with others."[6]

While technological advances offer a variety of benefits, there simply is no replacement for human interaction. No one will argue there isn't a *place* for technology that makes our life operate with less "friction"—the term used for a physical or psychological hindrance that interrupts a user's experience—but a "frictionless" experience can be problematic.

Nicholas Epley, professor of behavioral science at the University of Chicago Booth School of Business, stated, "I think the real danger of the frictionless economy is that at any moment it's easier to do the non-social thing." Isolation and humans, as we learned in 2020, is not a healthy combo.

Researchers have "repeatedly found that people wildly overestimate the friction, the awkwardness they will feel if forced to engage with others. . . . At the same time, they wildly underestimate how good they, and the people they meet, will feel afterward."[7]

Don't get me wrong, I love online grocery shopping as much as the next person, but the truth is, with each hour I *save,* I might actually be missing out. A study published in the fall of 2021 showed that "despite our fears of awkwardness, deep, meaningful conversations with strangers are not only easier than expected but also left participants feeling better about themselves."[8]

I've witnessed this human-connection lift many times, but perhaps none so pronounced as on an otherwise forgettable Saturday morning. My husband, Michael, usually handles ballet pickup on Saturdays, and, unbeknownst to me, every week he and my daughter like to stop by the food truck on the corner and get a donut after class. One Saturday, Michael was out of town so I was in charge of ballet pickup, and I became aware of the ritual only after my daughter approached the truck window and was about to order a glazed donut (her third favorite, she informed me, after chocolate glazed and vanilla glazed).

Without much choice, or real reason to protest, I nodded and she placed her order with the man in the window. I thanked him and handed him my card.

"Oh," he said. "We're cash only."

He could tell by the look on my face that I was currently "card only." Without hesitation, he handed me the donut bag through the window.

"It's OK. Get me next time. I know you . . ." He paused. "Well. I know *her*."

His eyes twinkled as he smiled at my freckle-faced daughter. She smiled back.

As we walked home, my daughter reveled in his kindness and, though she didn't have the words for it, the comfort of community and connection—the invaluable sense that around the various corners and out of the small windows in a big city, there are people looking out for you. With bits of glaze on her lips she named him "Uncle Donut," and when we got home she tucked an envelope in her dance bag with cash for two donuts. One for this Saturday and one for the Saturday to come.

Could we have ordered donuts from Dunkin' via my phone and grabbed them from the pickup window without encountering another human? Certainly. But for all the dopamine hits available on a screen, reward points from an app, there is nothing quite like sharing a moment with another person.

Far from inconveniences, encounters with other humans "are one of the most important resources we have," says David Sax, author of the book *The Future is Analog: How to Create a More Human World.*[9]

A world that is becoming increasingly "streamlined," where a person can go to work, exercise, and eat all their meals for months at a time in the privacy of their home without seeing another human, is not necessarily a world in which our lives are better.

That lack of connection is more likely *contributing* to a widespread leadership crisis. When it comes to leading a team and thriving as an organization, less human does *not* equal more success. Getting ahead will require becoming more *human* and tapping into the one thing that has *always been* our unique advantage: *storytelling.*

THE RAPID CHANGE OR ELSE MANIA VS. THE RAPID CHANGE TRUTH

You've probably heard the phrase "Move fast and break things." Attributed to Mark Zuckerberg, it was the internal motto of Facebook until 2014. Since then, Facebook's slogan has evolved, changing to "Move fast and build things" to "Move fast with stable infra" to "Move fast" to "Move fast and please, please, please don't break anything" to, most recent, "Move fast together."[10]

What *hasn't* changed in these slogans? The stated need to "move fast." It makes sense:

No matter where we live, what our age, our current role or destination, there is a distinct sense that we need to **hurry up**. Even if what we're racing toward or from isn't exactly clear, that doesn't stop us from pedaling as fast as we can just to keep up, much less to get ahead.

And though we can't really opt out of "moving fast" when it is the universally accepted pace . . . getting caught up in the chaos of the moment will only lead to more chaotic moments.

Is it possible that we've gotten *move fast* all wrong? That we've created an environment where the ink doesn't have time to dry on one headline before a new one renders it almost obsolete? Think about it. There was a time in the not-too-distant past when the phrase "That didn't age well" referred to a statement or fashion trend or piece of pop culture from a decade earlier. Or if not a decade, then at least a year. A week? Even now, it can be a couple of hours.

Like one afternoon in March 2023 when I was on the phone with a friend who works in banking. We were discussing how things seem to be changing all the time and she said, with a bit of relief in her voice, "Well. It's times like these I'm grateful I work in banking, where the day-to-day is pretty predictable."

Not even two hours later the *Shark Tank* rerun I was watching was interrupted with breaking news: Silicon Valley Bank had collapsed, rendering our conversation and her statement obsolete. (I texted her the headline and an eyes-open-wide-shocked emoji, and she responded with an eye-roll + palm-to-face emoji combo.)

To be honest, nothing, not even the most innocuous statements, ages very well anymore (and no amount of injections can salvage this type of wrinkle in time). The relentless, rapid change has people of all ages longing for the good ol' days—wishing things to go back to the better, easier, simpler way they were, "even though we didn't know it at the time," wrote Suzy Welch, professor of management practice at New York University's Stern School of Business, in a recent article about Gen Z in the workplace.[11]

The sentiment was so pervasive, in fact, that after declaring "photobomb" and "binge-watch" (how lighthearted and benign these words are!) the "Words of the Year" in 2014 and 2015, respectively, *The Collins English Dictionary* announced the defining Word of the Year for 2022 as:

> *Permacrisis.*
>
> [permacrisis (ˈpɜːməˌkraɪsɪs) an extended period of instability and insecurity, esp. one resulting from a series of catastrophic events]

It's no surprise that the permacrisis affects not only morale but also the mental health of people in the workforce. It contributes to absenteeism and "quiet quitting," or an employee doing the bare minimum at work, not taking on or being interested in new roles or responsibilities, failing to speak up in meetings, and more. One study of employees at two universities in Thailand confirmed that even *perceived* uncertainties resulted in mental exhaustion. But, of course, uncertainty existed long before 2022 and before the word "permacrisis" was coined, affecting job performance and mental health and well-being.

Perhaps even more damaging, this state of permacrisis strips away confidence, leaving leaders flailing in the wind. Some compensate for this lack of confidence by overreacting and responding too quickly to problems that present themselves, making extreme or unwise choices. Others become indecisive or forfeit long-term success for short-term wins. They look for the quickest fixes and fall for "too good to be true" solutions (or manias) out of desperation to get ahead or, at the very least, not miss out.

However, and contrary to popular belief, we cannot overcome chaos using the very things that created the chaos in the first place.

THE RAPID CHANGE TRUTH IS . . .

The fastest we've *ever* done *anything* was thirty-five thousand to seventy-five thousand years ago. Now, it's unlikely that when Mr. Zuckerberg first coined his infamous motto he was thinking back thousands of years to when the first stories were told, but he might as well have been. As we discussed at the very beginning of this book, stories broke the rules of evolution such that humans could "move fast" past entire levels of natural selection. Humans will always bend, whether they want to admit it or not, to the power of a story. As important as you may already suspect the ability to craft a compelling story to be, it's only going to become *more* essential—not only as a skill, but as a perspective, an approach.

Despite all the crazy advances and rapid changes we chase . . . in this very important way, humans have not changed.

Food.

Water.

Shelter.

Story.

Yes, business will change. Markets will rise and fall. Technologies will evolve. Anyone who tells you they know what is ahead is lying. No one knows. And even the best predictions are just that: predictions.

But there is something that will remain true, despite any and all transformations we experience in business, culture, and innovation: Story is an essential part of being human. There is an opportunity here for those who choose to see it. An opportunity—even at the rapid speed of modernization and development, despite AI and uncertainty—to remember what made *Homo sapiens* so powerful in the first place: stories.

What business (and the world!) needs now is people who can *create environments of calm in the chaos.* Leaders who can connect with their team members and customers, in authentic ways versus automated ones. The wisest leaders will get good at story while everyone else is distracted by the newest trend or hiding from the latest dire warning or market flux. They will invest as much effort into the application of the original evolutionary advantage, *storytelling*, as they do into the adoption and integration of new technologies and ways of work.

MANAGING THE MANIA

While certainly exploring new trends, technologies, endeavors, and approaches is essential to both your personal evolution and the growth of your organization, getting swept up in the insanity that has become the definitive nature of work as we know it can also mean getting swept away. Or at the very least, letting the noise and movement of the crowd distract you from the truths that truly move business forward.

I became familiar with Tulipmania via the abovementioned Michael, my husband.

He became familiar with Tulipmania when he stumbled upon the mania while searching for the resale value of—if you can believe it—tulip bulbs.

You see, every April we watch in awe and wonder as the Park Avenue median in New York City bursts to life in a sea of tulips. Each year they are a different color—one year red, one year yellow, one year a deep royal purple. They are *so* beautiful it almost makes sense why people went so crazy for them. Almost.

And then, every May, once the final petals of the tulips have fallen, there is a designated day when you can *dig up the bulbs* and plant them in your own garden for the following spring. People run to the median with all variety of digging tools—cups, spatulas, wine glasses . . . very few actual shovels or trowels—and by the following morning, miles of median has returned to dirt and the bulbs are with their new owners. One of whom was, indeed, Michael. Which is why he was searching the internet for the going rate for a tulip bulb.

"What if we collected a whole bunch of them and then sold them online?" he asked. "We could brand them *Park Avenue Tulips*! We could sell them by color and year. I think people would pay a lot for them!"

I told him he sounded crazy.

He sent me Tulipmania.

In particular, he sent me a link to a book published in 1852, *Memoirs of Extraordinary Popular Delusions and the Madness of*

Crowds, with a foreword by Bernard Baruch, financier and advisor to presidents. Baruch amassed a great fortune in the New York Stock Exchange and claimed the perusal of the *Delusions and Madness* book had saved him millions. In his foreword Baruch shared this quote: "Anyone taken as an individual is tolerably sensible and reasonable— as a member of a crowd, he at once becomes a blockhead."[12]

Don't be a blockhead.

Be suspicious of the crowd.

Steer clear of the mania.

And start with putting story first.

TWO

But First, Story

"The most powerful person in the world is the storyteller."
—STEVE JOBS

There was a time when you couldn't walk into a fitness class or endure a morning school drop-off session without seeing the phrase "But First, Coffee." It was printed on shirts, mugs, trucker hats, and sandwich boards outside any local establishment that might serve the essential elixir. That's not to mention the digital prevalence.

The expression is credited to designer and illustrator Topher McCulloch, who reportedly coined the phrase when he "reblogged" a Tumblr photo of a well-designed office space posted by his friend Colin Quinn in 2010. Looking at the image of the office, it's nice. There is color, light, and lots of spaces for storage . . . and apparently it was ideal enough for McCulloch to comment on it.

McCulloch captioned the reblogged photo:

"Maybe it's a good day for rearranging the office/dining room. But first, coffee."

According to McCulloch, the tossed-off phrase meant that he was feeling lazy at that moment and needed a boost. Who can relate to needing a boost? A lot of people. Google searches for the phrase skyrocketed shortly after Quinn and McCulloch created graphic images of the quote, and eventually the phrase became ubiquitous.

Anything is possible. But first, coffee.[1] Or if not coffee, then maybe something else. In time, many other "But firsts . . ." emerged. But First, Matcha. But First, Tea. There were tank tops with "But First, Yoga." Or "But First, Tacos." Or "But First, Champagne." Some people prefer to But First, Run. Or But First, Meditation. Some But First, Tennis, or (despite the typography challenge it presents) But First, Pickleball. And though a search for "But First, Gardening" yielded no results, a related "But First, Weed" seemed popular.

It's a simple sentiment—needing one thing in order to effectively handle whatever awaits you next. And regardless of your preferred "but first" fuel for starting or getting through the day, when it comes to leadership and facing challenges in business, the phrase I want you to focus on is:

BUT FIRST, STORY.

Before you do *anything*, before you make a decision, before you take action, before you ask a question of a colleague or customer, before you invest in a new technology, consider the *story* first. Ask yourself:

What is the story here?

What piece of the story am I missing?

What could the story be?

What story needs to be told?

What story does my team need to hear?

What story am I currently, at this very moment, in the middle of, and how might that story end?

CEOs and leaders have accepted that technical skills alone are not sufficient to accelerate growth and overcome obstacles. Modern business challenges will require more nuanced, human skills like empathy, inclusive leadership, interpersonal communication, agility, and resilience. Areas of high focus include attracting and retaining talent and developing the next generation of leaders.[2]

As evidence of this mindset shift, an article in *Forbes* listed the top ways CEOs could get back on track if they had struggled the year before. You'll see I've added, in brackets, a few words that help to underscore the story-point.

Here are ways CEOs can "get back on track":

1. Tap Into Emotional Intelligence Skills [by Sharing Stories]

2. Reconnect the Company to Your Mission [by Telling Stories]

3. Authentically Connect with Employees [by Sharing Your Stories]

4. Prioritize Building Trust Among Employees [Best Done by Exchanging Stories]

5. Discover What Inspires You First [and Revisit Your Life Stories]

6. Be Honest and Demonstrate Empathy [by Sharing Even the Unpleasant, Embarrassing Stories]

7. Own the Challenges without Spin [and Face Your Stories]

8. Gain Buy-In by Acting on Employees' Suggestions [by Listening to Their Stories]

9. Be Open, Humble, and Courageous [through Storytelling]

10. Recognize Employees' Value [by Taking a Moment to Hear Their Stories]

11. Help People See the Point of Inflection [by Telling Illustrative Stories]

12. Connect Corporate Goals to Personal Goals [by Telling Stories]

13. Use the Past as a Learning Experience to Grow [When Seeking to Understand Your Story]

14. Give Employees the Opportunity to Discuss Pain Points [and Listen to Their Stories][3]

At the risk of sounding like Michael Scott from *The Office* who mutters "That's what she said" under his breath at least once an episode, you really can add a phrase about "story" to the end of any one of the items listed and transform it from a *suggestion* to a *course of action*.

Seek the Story. Share the Story. Tell the Story. Ask for the Story. Hear the Story. The most important business challenges facing executives today, and those that will likely continue to plague them in the years to come, can all be solved by putting story at the center of the strategy. And in doing so, transform from the outdated, insufficient, previously acceptable shell of "a leader" into one who can manage the intricacies of a changing, nuanced, more aware world of work—a Story Forward Leader.

THE STORY FORWARD LEADER

I think the first articulation of what I call the Story Forward Leader came from my husband during an attempt to trick me. It was movie night in our household and, with one preteen boy and one preteen girl, the options for "movies that we'll all enjoy" are limited.

My son and husband were pushing hard for a fantasy/action movie about a kid who was the last surviving being with the ability to control all four elements—fire, water, earth, and air.

"He's the last airbender!" my son exclaimed.

Knowing that wouldn't be enough to persuade me, my husband continued, "He has the ability to use something as common as air to bring the nations together and save the world . . . much like storytelling! Leaders who master the overlooked power of story and the ones who will lead their companies to greatness . . ."

My husband held his breath as I deliberated.

"Fine," I said with a sigh. Maybe I would gain some allegorical insight.

One hundred and three minutes later, though the movie itself was terrible (the second and third movies in the trilogy were canceled) and though Michael's intentions may not have been entirely pure, he wasn't wrong. A movie about the ability to master something as ubiquitous as air and turn an unsuspecting human, a child even, into a visionary savior of the people, is exactly the story I am seeking to tell.

Those who can master stories, like those who can bend air, are the leaders we need right now. Yes, there are facts and figures that companies and leadership performance are measured against. And then there is that invisible, irresistible, can't-quite-put-your-finger-on-it quality that some people possess or exude, or both. Those for whom the waters seem to part, the people seem to follow, struggles that snag others and hinder their progress bead up like water on a waterproof jacket and evaporate. Their teams are more effective, they even *enjoy* showing up and working hard. These are just a few of the identifiable benefits of becoming a Story Forward Leader.

And the results of this approach are undeniable.

THE FAIR MARKET VALUE OF A STORY

On April 6, 2017, the *New York Times* published an article titled "Tesla Has Something Hotter Than Cars to Sell: Its Story." (And if you didn't think I cut this article out and have saved it for seven years, did you not read about my newspaper hoarding?) To say a lot has happened in the years since the article was published would be an understatement as expansive as outer space.

Look, love him or hate him, Musk understands the power of a story.

The text on the worn, yellowed newspaper reads, "Tesla has ascended into a rarefied realm of so-called story stocks—companies that have so bewitched investors that their stock prices are impervious to any traditional valuation measures because their stories are simply too good not to be true . . ."[4] It mentioned that Ford and General Motors are likely "tearing their hair out in frustration" because of Tesla's stock surge, while their shares were dropping.

The article quotes Tesla's market value at $49 billion.

In the fall of 2021, the value was $1.2 trillion.

The day this chapter was written, the market value was $502 billion.

And yes. The difference between the second two numbers is a loss. But I would argue the more interesting story is the difference between the first number and the last. In six years, even with multiple global crises, a variety of PR nightmares (a photo with a sink? An unbreakable window shattering onstage?), an explosive foray into space, and many, many more ups and downs, each of which, on their own, could have been The End . . . and the company's value grew—ten times.

Whatever your feelings about the man, Musk has managed to bend air and change business as we know it. And the secret as to how was right there, in that headline, oh so long ago.

A STORY IN THE WRONG HANDS

Before we continue, I need to address an important but unfortunate reality of the power of the Story Forward. While it is certainly my hope that this concept finds its way into the hands of as many world-changers as possible, it comes with one, distinct risk: the power of the Story Forward in the wrong hands can have devastating results. Because yes, just as there is a dark side to the Force in *Star Wars*, there is, too, a dark side to storytelling. It can be mastered and used for good or mastered and used for no-good—think

Sam Bankman-Fried (crypto fraudster), Elizabeth Holmes (formerly a biochemical phenom, currently incarcerated in federal prison).

Those who master the Story Forward approach can become *so* compelling that the basic lines of questioning—Are the numbers you're claiming to have real? Does the thing you're trying to sell us even exist?—seem irrelevant, causing even the "most intelligent," "most risk-averse" to throw money at the story. A lot of money—some to the tune of $175 million.

As was the case for Charlie Javice.

Javice, named to *Forbes'* list of 30 Under 30 in 2019, is the "fintech prodigy" who, in April 2023, was freed on a $2 million bond. She had been arrested at Newark Airport and was forced to surrender her passports after being accused of duping the behemoth JPMorgan Chase into buying her company, Frank, for $175 million.

Frank promised to be the "Amazon" of financial aid, saving students money and dignity when trying to achieve the American dream of higher education. Javice shared her own struggle with financial aid and paying for college.

"Ms. Javice's personal story—and pledge to cut through the painful thicket of government forms, jargon and regulations surrounding the aid process—must have made compelling reading for angel investors and venture capitalists."[5]

She shared how tortuous, frustrating, and time-consuming it was. "It's grueling, it's emotional," Javice was quoted as saying, adding that her mother was "in tears" during several phone conversations with the financial aid office.[6]

Let's pause for a moment here. Do you know what Javice's parents did for a living? It seems relevant, since the central part of Charlie Javice's story was the struggle to access financial aid year after year in order to pay for higher education.

Her father worked on Wall Street for decades. Even his old business school friends wondered how their finance buddy's daughter would ever qualify for financial aid. Maybe that was the frustration? Charlie couldn't get financial aid because her parents were too wealthy? That changes the tone of the story a bit, don't you think?

Though the bank has not commented on their process of due diligence when it came to Javice and her story, one can only assume JPMorgan Chase's team, many of whom have little real-world experience or knowledge of how the financial aid process actually works (so removed that one might even confuse FAFSA with a video game about soccer), liked the story. Loved it, even. So much so that "the bank planned to pay her a $20 million retention fee if she stuck around for a stretch of time after the merger closed."[7]

But after sending *one* email to 400,000 addresses in Frank's database of millions of (later falsified) customers, only a small percentage of the emails were even able to be delivered, resulting in clicks from only 103 recipients. You don't have to be a digital marketing guru to know that open rate is worse than abysmal . . . it's embarrassing.

Javice, like countless fraudsters who have gone before her, knew the power of a story, and she exploited it.

That is not airbending; that is lying.

Do not make me regret telling you about the power of a story.

Do not lie.

EVERY PROBLEM IS A STORY PROBLEM

Now that that's established, let's get back to airbending.

If one tenet to becoming Story Forward is "But first, Story," another essential tenet is this:

Every problem is a story problem.

Every challenge is a story and can be solved through story.

The good news is, stories are an unlimited resource. You are *made* of stories. Your *team* is made of people made of stories, who are now joined together and have *shared* stories. The company you work for (or own, or otherwise engage with) is made of stories. There are stories from the past. And there are stories happening right now that will be stories you will tell in the future.

Throughout this book, we will discuss many of the business challenges that are top of mind and tip of tongue more in depth. But it all starts here.

Every problem is a story problem. More specifically, every problem:

1. *has* a story,

2. *needs* a story, and/or

3. *is* a story in the process of being told.

From this point forward, we will refer to these ideas as the Three Truths in Story Forward leadership. They are simple statements that, if a leader commits to considering when faced with any business challenge, have the ability to unlock the most human solutions.

We will dive in, much deeper, in subsequent chapters, but I want to introduce you to these three Truths here.

TRUTH 1:
THERE IS ALWAYS A STORY

Think: "There is more to the Story" and "What is the Story?"

The first Truth reminds you that whenever there is a problem or a conflict, there is a story at work that you may not be aware of. You'll be better equipped to solve the problem if you figure out what the story is, and in order to do *that,* you have to be aware that there could be an unknown, untold story there.

If you've ever felt the need for better decision-making or for more empathy in the office, Truth 1 is how you get there. And it must start with the baseline awareness of the storied nature of life.

A Story Forward Leader knows that there is always a story, there is never *not* a story. If you think for a moment that maybe there isn't a story at play, it simply means the story is buried, or disguised, or hidden away—stuffed in the back of an office closet, or a cubicle desk drawer, or lurking in the Slack channel or whispered around the watercooler. Curiosity and the genuine desire to seek out the stories you don't yet know are critical.

Additionally, Story Forward Leaders are not afraid of the stories they may find. A Story Forward Leader does not try to avoid stories that might illustrate points or perspectives that are different than their own. A Story Forward Leader knows that more stories lead to deeper understanding, and with deeper understanding comes more opportunity for achieving greatness.

Someone who takes a story-first approach has this Truth on repeat anytime they're faced with a roadblock, obstacle, or something that just doesn't make sense:

This problem . . . it has a story.

This person . . . it (he/she/they) has a story.

This point of confusion . . . it has a story.

This unexplained behavior . . . it has a story.

And *I* need to figure out what that story is so we can all move onward and upward.

TRUTH 2:
A STORY NEEDS TO BE TOLD

Think: "I should tell a story here" and "This calls for a story."

The second Truth focuses on the more common expression of storytelling in business. Discussed in depth in my first book, *Stories That Stick: How Storytelling Can Captivate Customers, Influence Audiences, and Transform Your Business,* storytelling is the most effective form of communication when attempting to bridge the gaps in business.

From sales and marketing to presentations and pitches—storytelling brings messages to life, makes them memorable, and makes them matter more.

However, the power of telling a story extends beyond better marketing copy. Telling stories is a pathway for leader transparency, an expression of authenticity, and a way to connect team members back to why they do what they do. Using stories can increase ROI and help close sales, and it is also a way to increase creativity, engagement, and more compelling oratory.

Essential to activating this Truth is leaders' willingness to "own" their own stories. A Story Forward Leader doesn't hide from their stories, and though maybe they wished they had behaved, or acted, or decided better, they do not try to add filters to make the stories more appealing. They know that sometimes, the most powerful stories for leaders to tell are when lessons were learned the hard way. People know and can relate to leaders who admit that mistakes happen and that growth isn't always pretty in the moment.

It should also be said that *grace* and *humility* are required. Story Forward leadership is not permission for blatant self-aggrandizing. Yes, you're supposed to be telling stories. Yes, the team needs to hear them. But if each of your stories is about how awesome you are, you didn't understand the assignment. Oh. And again. The stories should be true. Duh.

Get this Truth right; your ability to influence and inspire is the pot of gold at the end of this Truth rainbow.

TRUTH 3:
YOU'RE ALWAYS IN THE MIDDLE
OF THE STORY

Think: "This isn't the beginning of the story and it's not the end" and "This is a story we will tell someday."

This third and final Truth of Story Forward leadership is the most nuanced. Mastery of this Truth is first an inside job with an outward expression that is less literal than the previous two Truths. It is the ability to maintain proper perspective. When things are going wrong, when there is chaos all around you and your team, when fear of failure and what it will cost is mounting, Truth 3 says: this, *too*, is a story, and I'm in the middle of it.

Truth 3 allows the leader to rise above the challenge or chaos. To not get dragged under or carried away by it. Not unlike an out-of-body experience, Truth 3 allows a leader to observe the chaos and take note—knowing that someday, it will be a story to tell. It is with this knowing that a leader can remain optimistic and resilient, and teach a team to do the same.

Like when Jamie Dimon, the chief executive of JPMorgan Chase, admitted on a quarterly earnings call that the acquisition of Javice's farce of a financial aid company was a huge mistake. However, not wallowing in embarrassment, he commented on CNBC, "There are always lessons—we always will make mistakes. . . . I tell our people, we make mistakes, it's OK, and when we know what all the lessons are, I'll tell you what they were."[8]

A STORY SOLUTION FOR EVERY PROBLEM

Ultimately, a Story Forward Leader knows that, in business, every problem is first and foremost a story problem. And as such, for every problem there is a story solution.

It could be a story that you don't yet know or understand (Truth 1), or the problem needs a story to be told in order to solve it (Truth 2), or the challenge is actually the middle of a story that you're in the process of living (Truth 3).

In any case, the following chapters are designed to help you master the power of these three Truths and, in doing so, gain access to some of the most important attributes great leaders are known to possess—more informed and robust decision-making, empathy, the ability to create connection and influence, to inspire, to maintain and create optimism, to raise resilient teams, and, as a result, to overcome the most challenging obstacles business leaders face.

THERE IS ALWAYS A STORY

How Seeking Out

Unknown Stories Leads to

Better Decisions and More

Empathetic Leaders

THREE

Know There's *Always* a Story (. . . and You Can Save the World!)

$$\times$$

"Millions saw the apple fall,
but Newton was the one who asked why."
—BERNARD BARUCH

"I think we ought to think of why the Russians did this."

Though it isn't John F. Kennedy's most famous quote, it is perhaps one of his most important.

It was October 19, 1962, and the Cuban Missile Crisis was already three days deep. At this point, the American population was unaware that just ninety miles from the coast of Florida was a threat that could catapult our world into nuclear war.

In the decades since the crisis, much has been dissected and written about the days when the world teetered on the brink of nuclear war, thoroughly examining those excruciating thirteen days with every political, psychological, linguistic microscope we have.

However, if there is one sentence that stands out . . . it is the one above.

> Let me just say a little . . . first about . . . what the problem is . . . from . . . at least from my point of view . . . I think we ought to think of why the Russians did this.[1]

It's important to note that it's not just the statement itself but rather the context in which it was stated that makes this sentence so important (and also may explain why Kennedy seemed hesitant and kept tripping over his words while saying it).

At this point in the crisis, Kennedy had been continuing much of his planned schedule, meetings, campaign events, while the Department of Defense's Joint Chiefs of Staff were gathering and analyzing any intel they could find.

"Mr. President, as you know, we've been meeting on this subject ever since we discovered the presence of missiles in Cuba . . ." began Joint Chiefs chairman General Maxwell Taylor, who then summarized the discussions thus far.

"From the outset I would say that we felt we were united on the military requirement: we could not accept Cuba as a missile base; that we should either eliminate or neutralize the missiles there and prevent any others coming in.

"From a military point of view that meant three things. First, attack with the benefit of surprise those known missiles and offensive weapons that we knew about. Secondly, continued surveillance then to see what the effect would be. And third, a blockade to prevent the others from coming in. I would say, again, from a military point of view, that seemed clear. We were united on that . . ."[2]

General Taylor then recommended that the president "hear out" the other chiefs' comments on whether they should move forward with the full-on military plan or one that took some "political requirements" into consideration.

This was the moment when the young president, who had just six months earlier launched a failed attack to remove Fidel Castro from power and was no doubt, both inwardly and outwardly, recovering from the embarrassment, spoke up.

Clearly the Joint Chiefs had a lot of recommendations and courses of action, but had anyone considered the *rest of the story*?

I think we ought to think of why the Russians did this.

What followed that statement was a long monologue by Kennedy who, at that moment, did not have the luxury of picking up the phone and calling the Kremlin to see what was going on. Instead, he considered aloud the various possible stories that might have led to this impossible crossroads. He started with one option and then said, "On the other hand . . ." followed by "On the other hand . . ." a few seconds later, and still one more "On the other hand . . ."—leaving a person to wonder just how many hands Kennedy had.

After verbally exploring all the possible storylines, Kennedy ultimately told the advisors he had made a decision. Though the advisors favored a more extreme approach, Kennedy said they would respond to the threat with a limited naval blockade. The chiefs fought back. Recordings of the meeting show General Curtis LeMay jumping aggressively into the discussion. He declared that the United States didn't have "any choice except direct military action." LeMay then went straight for psychological destruction, asserting that any other solution would be as shameful as the "appeasement at Munich," a reference to "their generation's ultimate metaphor for cowardice."[3]

Much has been written about the thirteen days that made up the Cuban Missile Crisis. Over time, the release of recordings and information has led to more analysis and insight into the decisions and the process by which they were made. However, whether it was strategy, arrogance, luck, or a little of each, history might look a lot different if the president had not taken a moment to consider what the rest of the story might be.

The act—of considering that there might be more to the story than what is immediately presented or available—is a valuable leadership asset.

So valuable, in fact, you and I might be *alive* today to even consider its value *because* of its value.

Therein lies the power of Truth 1 in our Story Forward approach to leadership.

TRUTH 1:
THERE IS ALWAYS A STORY

There is a story behind every challenge. There is a story behind every success. There is a story (many, many stories) within every person. There are stories that are obvious; there are stories that are subtle. Anytime something doesn't quite make sense or things are moving along one way and take a sudden turn—there is a piece of the story you don't know. There is never *not* a story, even if—initially—you can't see it. And that story affects everything.

Imagine a stellar sales rep who received a scathing complaint from a customer and whom the heads of the company told the rep's manager to terminate immediately. Yes, customer satisfaction is important. And yes, the allegations appeared to be true. However, the manager (who sent me this true-life example) had this Truth in his mind: "*There's a story here . . .*" and he knew that they would all be better off if he figured out what it was.

Despite the pressure from above, the manager worked to uncover the rest of the story and sure enough, it was simply a huge misunderstanding. The rep stayed, and the manager was spared losing a top performer and damaging team morale.

It is through this Truth—*There is always a story*—that better decisions are made. Not necessarily faster, but better. It is through the act of second-guessing (in the positive sense), that we gain an opportunity for greater understanding so that our actions lead us forward instead of in circles. This truth offers a clear pathway to activate empathy, which allows for connection in an increasingly disconnected world. This truth will help leaders develop other leaders and create environments that are rich in inclusion and belonging.

None of this should come as a surprise—we've all heard that "knowledge is power," and any child of the 1990s will remember the nostalgic four-tone chime of the "*The more you know*" television campaigns. However, I feel obligated to warn you, and disgusted to tell you, that while '90s fashion has made a comeback, the necessary art of seeking the story seems to have gone completely, dangerously out of style.

THE PLIGHT (AND CALL) OF AN
HONORABLE, UNFASHIONABLE PURSUIT

There's a word that stands out in the two previous stories of this chapter—*pressure.*

The *pressure* from Kennedy's advisors to take action. The *pressure* that the heads of the company put on the manager to immediately terminate the valuable employee. Blame cancel culture, blame how fast news can spread in the age of the internet, blame the hordes who "want answers now" . . . regardless of where you point the finger, the fact remains: A leader, taking a moment to consider that there might be more to the story than what is currently known, runs counter to everything the modern media, the boards of directors, and the entrepreneurial gurus currently stand for. Pressure is a double-edged sword that, while it can absolutely *make* you, you yourself have no doubt felt how it can also *break* you.

Take the famed former news anchor of Televisa, Mexico's largest television company, Denise Maerker.

In 2005, Maerker was working for a small upstart network where her guests, including politicians, were uncharacteristically unfiltered, when a story broke. It involved footage of police officers storming a ranch and arresting two people accused of kidnapping for ransom. While producers and viewers were glued to the footage and assumed they knew the story, Maerker investigated further . . . and caught wind that perhaps there was actually much *more* to the story. And she sought to find it.

As a result of her curiosity and reporting, it was revealed that the footage was not real, but rather a reenactment: a staged publicity stunt. Her willingness to find the rest of the story shot her to superstardom, ultimately landing her the job at Televisa where she became the most-watched news anchor in Mexico, with three times as many viewers as her closest competitors.

Maerker's ascendency could be classified as a quintessential success story for implementing Truth 1. A commitment to resisting the temptation to make snap judgments and instead seeking to know the whole story enables an unlikely middle-aged (strike one) female (strike two) to rise above the rest to become the coveted prime-time nightly newscast host and a household name.

I only wish the story could end there.

But, in January 2023, her insatiable desire to know the whole story led to Maerker stepping down as Televisa's on-air host.

You see, the news climate had changed dramatically since she started. Maerker's restrained style—her practice of listening versus battling, asking versus engaging, her method of reporting driven by curiosity and the inclination to hear the story instead of driving a certain agenda—had become her undoing. Analysts said she was too timid, and even her own mother called the station to complain about Maerker's unbiased coverage.

Perhaps it would better suit *my* agenda to leave this part of the story out. To *not* tell you that Truth 1—*There is always a story*—is a truth that many find unacceptable. So much so, in fact, that several years ago I posted a quote on one of my social media accounts that said, "There is always more to a story," and, though not confirmed by the platform, the post appeared to be shadow-banned (the practice of the platform making posts and content invisible to users/followers). Like even the *concept* shouldn't be uttered.

In rapidly changing, even polarizing times, the pressure to "make statements" and "take immediate action" overrides, even erases, the subtler, more objective, more curious approach. Maerker saw the proverbial writing on the wall. "There is going to be less and less space for people like me," she said.[4]

And we, in business and beyond, are worse for it.

It's true. There does seem to be less and less space for leaders who welcome the uncomfortable pause while the rest of the information is revealed. Leaders who take their time—despite their emotions or interests—to seek to understand the story better. Perhaps exploring the rest of the story would lead to the same conclusions or courses of action, but the discipline of discernment alone has value.

This is a lost art—to some it's a threatening one—but it is necessary. We *need* more leaders who don't fear asking questions and learning more. Who don't assume they already know the story or ignore that there's a story to be known in the first place.

Sensing there's a story there and seeking to find it is part of what gave humans our original edge. Like a sixth sense, an intuition that there was more to know. Whereas *now*, our intuition is often our undoing. And research shows it can drive us to *violate* this truth instead of living it.

THE LURE OF INTUITION

My in-laws have a sailboat. It's a forty-foot Catalina with two bedrooms, two bathrooms, and the oh-so-sexy name of . . . *Intuition*. I will admit, I seriously debated using the word "sexy" to describe something relating to my in-laws, but really, there just wasn't a better way to say it. I love the name—it seems mysterious and magical. Like it knows a secret that no one else in the harbor does.

And it's no wonder I have a positive association with the word. Intuition implies "knowing" versus "having to spend time figuring out." Intuition is efficient, and humans are extremely impatient. Not just when we're waiting for the light to change or when the person in line in front of us is taking forever, but we're impatient with ambiguity in general.

The potential to quickly tie up loose ends seems to be one of the primary functions of intuition. Leaders can rely on a combination of experience (and, let's face it, a little bit of magic) without having to waste time deep-diving into boring details or consulting with other team members. They can "go with their gut" and move confidently forward in no time flat.

However, when it comes to highly complex and changeable environments, research and history have proven intuition to be a dangerous shortcut. Relying on intuition can narrow the thinking of the leader, cut out valuable insight from the group, and lead to "intuition bias"—an often unreliable, irrational preference toward the *first* information we receive on a particular subject even when other information undermines the intuition's validity.[5] So strong is this bias, researchers have shown that even if the leader *does* take the time to consider, process, and understand all relevant information available in the immediate context, the intuition, right or wrong, will likely hold.

Read that last line again.

Right or wrong, the intuition will likely hold . . .

This kind of rigidity is exactly what we *don't* need in positions of power.

I understand. It's hard to resist the lure of intuition. I, too, have had moments where my intuitions were proven right and the self-satisfaction washed over me with an intoxicating warmth (not to mention I am a Pisces which, according to my daughter, who's newly obsessed with astrology, means I'm even more intuitively inclined). But regardless of your astrological sign, whether you are JFK on the third day of a thirteen-day global catastrophe with the fate of the world hanging in the balance, or you are an executive leading in the age of permacrisis, the best instinct to trust is the one that tells you there is more to the story.

As you'll read in the following chapters, now is the time for *curious* leaders. For those who take an extra (albeit unpopular) moment to seek the story while making decisions and guiding a team.

FOUR

More Stories = Better Decisions

"Sometimes reality is too complex. Stories give it form."
—JEAN-LUC GODARD

In the 1999 cult classic film *Office Space*, one of the employees, Tom, laments what he and his fellow coworkers need to do to escape their abysmal, soul-sucking cubicle life. He says they simply need to come up with one great idea. Just one. Like the pet rock. Come up with one great idea, he proposes, to make millions and break free of the shackles of humdrum employment. Then Tom says he already *has* a million-dollar idea: he calls it a "Jump to Conclusions" mat.

"It would be this mat that you would put on the floor, and it would have different *conclusions* written on it that you could *jump* to." Tom smiles as he waits for his colleagues' reactions. They are not impressed.

And while a mat for conclusions to jump to may be the "worst idea I've ever heard," as one of Tom's colleagues deems it, the pressure to make decisions that match the breakneck pace at which business is operating leaves leaders feeling like they have little choice but to jump. Even as decisions get more complicated, more and more corporate executives—45 percent, one study found—are relying more on instinct than on facts and figures.[1]

Before we dive into the *There is always a story* strategies Story Forward Leaders use to enhance decision-making, let's take a look at how we got here in the first place.

THE INVENTION OF "DECISION-MAKING"

In 1954, just a few short years before the thirteen days where the fate of the world depended on one man's decision, a retired telephone executive named Chester Barnard published the book *The Functions of the Executive*. It was in this book that it's believed the phrase "decision-making" was born. It articulated a preference for *action* over *deliberation* and added a "new crispness of action and desire for conclusiveness" that had not been previously expressed. The phrase signaled an element of power—denoting the end of deliberation and the beginning of action.[2]

Whether or not the Joint Chiefs advising Kennedy during the Cuban Missile Crisis had read the book, the frustration they expressed as Kennedy insisted on a path that would buy them more time to gain insight certainly signaled a preference for action over careful consideration and more information.

Further expressing the preference for speed, American sociologist Amitai Etzioni bemoaned the shortcomings of drawn-out decision-making: "Old-fashioned decision making doesn't meet the needs of a world with too much information and too little time. So-called rational decision making, once the ideal, requires comprehensive knowledge of every facet of a problem, which is clearly impossible today."[3]

By the way, the "today" he spoke of was 1989.

Even back then, information overload forced an approach where executives had no choice but to reject "reflection and analysis and instead charge full speed ahead and remake the world rather than seek to understand it."[4] Not only are leaders *called* to move full steam ahead, they are often *celebrated* for doing so. I mean, who doesn't love a genius who can make big decisions in small amounts of time?

When it works, great! But when it doesn't? Well . . .

THE SOUR SNAPPLE DEAL

In 1994, everything looked pretty good for Quaker Oats CEO William Smithburg. He was sixteen years into the job, leading the organization through frequent strategic upheavals, and he was regarded on Wall Street as a "top-notch executive who had done a good job of expanding new product niches . . . while keeping Quaker competitive in areas like cold cereals."[5]

So, when it was announced in November of that year that Quaker Oats would purchase Snapple, the tea and juice drinks brand, Smithburg no doubt felt confident that more success was inevitable.

After all, he had acquired Gatorade a decade earlier and made it into a superstar brand, and he was confident that Quaker could use its marketing power to repeat this feat with Snapple.

He bought Snapple . . . for $1.7 billion.

Which was fine . . . except that analysts estimated Snapple was worth a billion *less* than that.[6]

In fact, a *New York Times* article published earlier that summer mentioned the fact that Snapple was slowly losing market share while "battling PepsiCo over iced teas and Coca-Cola over fruit juices. The share price of Snapple stock has fluctuated wildly, and the company has tried to fend off several unsubstantiated rumors."[7] Up-and-coming brands like Arizona Beverages were gaining attention, and one expert predicted Snapple would be but a memory by the end of summer. "Popular perception is that Snapple died the moment Quaker touched it [but] the truth is it was already in a nosedive . . ."[8]

I don't know about you, but if I were looking to spend nearly two billion dollars and answered to an eagle-eyed group of investors, I would *at least* take a quick skim through the stacks of newspapers lying around the house for relevant articles. (Oh wait . . . that's right: newspapers lying around the house in piles is *my* thing.)

Nevertheless, combine a lack of due diligence with the failure to seek out the full Snapple story and, three years later, Quaker resold Snapple for less than one-fifth of the price it had paid.

Not only did Snapple produce "essentially a $1.4 billion hole in the balance sheet,"[9] but the mistake cost Smithburg his job.

Among investment bankers, to call a deal "a Snapple" has become shorthand for a gross strategic mistake. And Smithburg, one of the most experienced and admired executives in his industry, ultimately paid the price.[10]

Which begs the question: If one of the best in the business can make that kind of fatal decision, what is stopping the same fate from befalling the rest of us? What can be done in a world where fast decisions matter more than sound decisions and due diligence is quietly regarded as a flaw versus a strength?

Fortunately, knowing *there is always a story* enables a Story Forward Leader to counteract the constant pressure to "go fast" and recenter on the fact that intelligent decision-making, like most good things in life, requires sustained effort and at least a little exploration.

THE CASE FOR CURIOSITY

On March 4, 1916, the *Washington Post* published a story confirming the death of a cat named Blackie.[11] Blackie lived on the fifth floor at 203 West 130th Street in New York City. He had moved there with his human, Miss Mabel Godfrey, the previous summer. And while he preferred to stay inside, he was no less curious than other felines.

One ill-fated Tuesday afternoon, Blackie climbed into the fireplace. He had been known to do this; however, desiring more adventure, on this day he climbed up the flue and eventually became stuck atop the screen that separated the apartment flue from the main building chimney.

Though he cried for Miss Godfrey, he denied her attempts to lure him back down to safety and instead, on Wednesday, tried to climb higher but slipped and fell all the way down the chimney and was stuck on the first floor. Miss Godfrey spoke to the police department, the fire department, the health department, the building department, and finally the Washington Heights court, but alas, none of them were able to rescue Blackie. Finally, on Thursday morning, a plumber was able to access the chimney through the rear wall and pull Blackie out.

Blackie died ten minutes later. (May he rest in peace.)

So, there you have it. If you've ever wondered if the idiom was true, that if, despite their alleged nine lives, a cat could die of curiosity . . . it can. And Blackie appears to be the one that started the debate.

Of course, you are not a cat.

But that doesn't change the fact that curiosity might still feel risky. It requires asking questions and reveals that you don't know all the answers. And let's not forget the consequences of objectivity and deeper understanding, like those that befell Mexican reporter Maerker. However, look a bit more closely and you'll find signs pointing to the value, nay, the *necessity* of curiosity in changing times.

Study after study shows that there are positive correlations between leaders' "displayed levels of curiosity" and the success of their teams. In his dissertation, University of Arizona doctoral candidate Jonathan Evans found that, when leaders exhibited curiosity with their teams, there was a decrease in conflict among team members, teams were more creative, and projects were otherwise positively influenced.[12]

Another academic study looked at curiosity as a positive emotion in the general population and delved into its advantages in social relationships and feelings of well-being. The authors stated: "People who are regularly curious and willing to embrace the novelty, uncertainty, and challenges that are inevitable as we navigate the shoals of everyday life are at an advantage in creating a fulfilling existence compared with their less curious peers." The authors went on to claim that curious people even live longer than those who are less curious.[13]

Finally, in a recent article titled "Curiosity is a Leadership Superpower" published by Duke University's Corporate Education program (ranked number one globally), author Michael Bungay Stanier stated that engaging in curiosity as a "repeatable, deliberate behavior" is the pathway to smarter perception and action. "Stay curious and you will change the way you lead forever."[14]

Yes. Curiosity is a superpower, but don't overcomplicate it. It doesn't require you to wear a cape and tights. Sometimes, avoiding the pitfalls of modern decision-making is simply stepping back, in the heat of the moment, thinking to yourself: *there must be a story here that I'm missing.*

Here is a real example, sent to me, that I'm sure might sound familiar. A story of the kind of daily "fires" that leaders are expected to put out—and how a little curiosity regarding the rest of the story goes a long way.

AVOIDING A HUMONGOUS PROBLEM

It was a typical afternoon in the offices of Humongous Entertainment. Typical and also intense. As an award-winning game creator for children, especially in the early 2000s when games were all purchased in stores, deadlines were extremely important. If a game wasn't designed, manufactured, and on the shelves by fall, it would miss the holiday selling season, which, in truth, was the only season that mattered.

Brian Pulliam had been working at Humongous Entertainment for many years and had played a critical role in the development of many games, including Backyard Hockey—a hockey game designed for kids younger than twelve. Backyard Hockey, in addition to the standard pressure of selling a lot of product, involved an NHL licensing partnership, increasing the stakes and the need for sales to perform.

So when one of Pulliam's new, but senior art directors came to him in a panic, he knew it could be bad. And at first glance, it was. The art director told Pulliam that they needed to re-render all the art for the game. The process would be expensive; renderings are costly, not to mention time-consuming. And, if truly necessary, this could compromise the time line; they might not complete the game in time for fall shelving and holiday sell-through.

The new art director was very convincing and, between the two of them, he was the expert over Pulliam when it came to renderings. The intensity of the deadlines also fostered an environment that favored quick (sometimes too quick) decision-making.

However, something wasn't adding up. *Why would there need to be a complete redo of the art when it wasn't even final yet?* Pulliam knew there had to be more to the story. "Given my experience, I often had to back someone up from the solution to the actual problem," Pulliam recalled. "So I took a moment and asked more questions: 'Why do you think we need to do that?' 'What problem are you trying to solve?'"

By asking a few simple questions, Pulliam discovered that the art director didn't like the designs as they were, though he was hesitant to admit that at first. The team had put together something that didn't match his vision—the colors were all wrong, and as a result, he wanted to start over.

"The art is bad. It's bad art," the director said, upset.

When Pulliam asked to see the art to which the director was referring, Pulliam realized they were looking at a *draft*, not the final art.

"This is a draft! Because of the way we handle colors for the final art, the problem will resolve itself," Pulliam explained. In just two weeks, he assured the director, the problem would be gone, just by the nature of the process.

All told, it was a conversation that began in the hallway, moved to the art director's office, and took a total of five extra minutes. Five minutes to take a moment to understand the full story, identify it as a simple misunderstanding—not an actual problem—and it saved them three months and fifty thousand dollars of wasted render time. In the end, the game was well-received, got great reviews, and overall was a huge success.

Most important, it was delivered on time, thanks to Pulliam knowing there was more to the story and asking a few good questions. And while it might seem obvious that the way to discover hidden stories is, much like in the example above, to ask for them, remembering to do so in the heat of the moment is not always our first instinct.

This is particularly true when we fear what the story might be and when it is the leader's role in the story that is causing the problem in the first place. For that delicate conundrum, we have our first essential strategy for becoming more Story Forward.

STRATEGY #1:
IF YOU FEAR THE ANSWER,
ASK THE QUESTION

The worst thing about knowing that there is more to the story—if there is a problem or behavior from your team that you don't understand or something isn't working—is the truth that the "more to the story" could be about *you*.

The story that you're missing or the reason things seem hard *could* be because of something *you* as the leader did or said, like a decision you made that had reverberating and unintended negative effects. There's a chance that the whispers around the watercooler, the stories being told, are intentionally being kept from you. And as unpleasant as that might be, or as uncomfortable to face, avoiding those stories and letting them fester only creates more problems.

I'll give you an example. In 2022, one organization went through a variety of changes that included updating how its sales team was compensated. This added some insult to injury because, as an organization that saw a boost in sales during 2020 and 2021, revenue had begun to shrink in 2022, which was already putting a strain on commissions.

A few salespeople had left the organization, those who remained weren't happy, and the leadership was frustrated. Up until this point, the salesforce had been composed of reasonable people who understood, even *thrived* throughout the ups and downs of mostly commission work. Yeah, sales were lower; that was to be expected. Yeah, commissions changed; they had to shift to avoid mass layoffs. The leadership assumed the bad attitude and lack of motivation was strictly due to these circumstances that, while not ideal, were kind of out of their control.

For months there was a standoff. The leaders pushed messages like "Stop focusing on the negative" and "When the goin' gets tough, the tough suck it up and sell something." Meanwhile the bad attitude continued to permeate the salesforce. Something *had to* be going on.

Finally, one executive decided to investigate, to find out if there was more to the story. He reached out to one of the top producers and finally learned what was *really* happening.

Months earlier, one of the long-standing execs of the organization had left without any explanation to the salesforce. The guy was just *gone*. And the fact that the leadership team did little to explain *why* he was gone and *instead* brought in a different guy and made *him* the face of the company . . . well, the salesforce had no choice but to fill in the gaps with their *own* story.

The salesforce deduced that something was wrong in the organization that caused the longtime leader to leave. And, further, they thought that leadership was trying to cover it all up by distracting the sales team with a shiny new guy.

The executive was shocked. That's not at all how it had gone down. In his mind and what he knew to be true was that the original leader was elderly and wanted to quietly step back. The executive team didn't realize he was such an icon among the salesforce—in fact, they assumed quite the opposite; that the salesforce would be *excited* to see the fresh approach of their new, energetic front man.

All this time, it hadn't been about an unreasonable salesforce; it had been about the executive team mishandling an important transition which, in the absence of transparent communication (which we'll discuss in depth later) and the full story, signaled trouble.

In essence, the executive team messed up. They totally botched the personnel change, and the repercussions almost caused a crisis.

Though I would argue, having watched this situation from afar, that the bigger mistake—and one that so many leaders make—was not seeking out the *real* story because the one the executives believed it to be spared them any blame.

It's not comfortable to discover, as a leader, that something you did *caused* the problem you're trying to solve. However, you will *always* make better decisions if you know the wholeness of what the *real* story is.

STRATEGY #2:
PRESS PAUSE

For many years, a small public community college in the northeast was home to a beloved and respected dean of mathematics, Beatrice Frank. Beatrice was greatly admired for her ability to pause in order to hear the other side of a story before making a decision.

Like the time a faculty member came into the office in a fury, shouting that a required book was not available through the bookstore and, as a result, thirty of the 120 students did not have access to the text. This instructor was irate and claimed that the students were the innocent victims of an incompetent bookstore manager, who had caused problems before, and the mistreatment had to stop. The faculty member demanded *immediate action* regarding the bookstore manager so the students didn't continue to suffer. As far as the faculty member was concerned, this was a five-alarm fire, the root cause had been identified, and therefore the dean must act without pause.

But pause Beatrice did.

She knew the bookstore manager. She also knew things didn't always run smoothly. There had, indeed, been missing books and supplies in the past. She could have easily used this new textbook problem as the final nail in the coffin of the bookstore manager's job. However, Beatrice also knew that the bookstore manager, whom many complained about as being difficult to work with, had inherited big problems with processes and efficiency when she took the job, which likely contributed to any defensive behavior.

Instead of immediately jumping up with a pitchfork, Beatrice activated the power of the pause. The faculty member was right, this was a big problem . . . which meant it deserved a little more time in order to figure out if there was more to the story.

Beatrice went to meet the bookstore manager to see if she could shed light on the situation and, what do you know, there was a big story to tell. It turned out the textbook issue was *not* a bookstore issue, and certainly not the bookstore manager's issue. It was a problem that went all the way to the publisher. There was a nationwide shortage of these texts, and schools across the country were having issues getting copies.

However, because Beatrice paused and came to the manager seeking the story instead of blaming, the manager immediately got to work, calling *her* district manager, insisting on a solution, and eventually securing an online option (a novel idea pre-2020) for forty-five days until the text would be back in stock.

While other colleges struggled to access the texts, the "difficult" bookstore manager bent over backward to help the students quickly, much to the credit of the Story Forward leadership of Beatrice Frank.

SLOW DOWN, YOU CRAZY CHILD

"Don't mistake quick thinking for IQ. Rapid answers often reflect shallow reasoning. Data: smarter people are faster on easy problems but slower on hard ones. They know haste makes waste and they want to get it right. Refusing to trade accuracy for speed is a sign of intellect."

This is a quote that Adam Grant, renowned author and professor at the Wharton School, posted to his two million social media followers. In the caption he pointed to a research study and subsequent summary that highlighted "the importance of slower, more effortful thinking for solving difficult problems and making better decisions."[15]

The researchers found "that participants with higher intelligence scores took more time to solve difficult problems"[16] and that these slower solvers had higher synchrony between brain regions, which "allowed for better integration of evidence and more robust working memory."

It has long been believed that the smarter you are, the faster you think. I am reminded of my son, who admitted to rushing through a math test in elementary school because other kids were finishing before him and he didn't want to feel stupid. And yes, in the study Grant referenced, those with high intelligence were able to move rapidly through easy questions, but once the problems became more complex, their pace slowed so as not to sacrifice accuracy.

I am not saying abiding by Truth 1 will raise your IQ. I *am* saying, do as the intelligent do. If accuracy matters, it pays to slow down and seek out the rest of the story. Feel free to openly pause. Stare at the person, the one who is insisting on immediate action, for a moment. Ask for twenty-four hours or even twenty minutes, and feel confident in doing so. Story Forward Leaders take their time and avoid unnecessary pain and anguish that comes from acting too quickly—especially when it comes to working with "challenging people."

STRATEGY #3:
START SECOND-GUESSING YOURSELF

No, I'm not talking about the kind of second-guessing that leads to self-doubt and inaction. A simple strategy to becoming a Story Forward Leader is to challenge your own initial assumptions. Always believing *there is a story* that maybe you don't yet know requires checking your automatic reactions and biases both in big ways (political perspectives, race, religion, social issues) and in small, everyday ways.

Anytime you think you know the answer or what the reason is, take a moment and say these words to yourself:

But what else could it be?

Much like a child has no problem asking why, why, why, why . . . Truth 1 gives you the freedom and the responsibility to do the same.

Here's how this played out among a group of friends, and while it wasn't a work situation, you can see how second-guessing pushed past assumption.

The discussion on the table was of a recent interview between Buffalo Bills defensive back Damar Hamlin and sports journalist (and former NFL star) Michael Strahan. In the interview broadcast on *Good Morning America*, the two were discussing the highly dramatic incident earlier that season when, on January 2, 2023, Hamlin collapsed on the football field in a highly anticipated matchup with the Cincinnati Bengals. For what seemed like a lifetime, the medical staff administered lifesaving support until Hamlin was taken off the field in an ambulance.

The days that followed were tense as the football community (and many others) waited for any sign of progress or otherwise. Miraculously, and thanks to the skill of the medical professionals both on the field and in the hospital, not only did Hamlin survive cardiac arrest, an event that takes the lives of nearly half a million Americans each year, but he was able to attend what would be the Bills' final game of the 2022–2023 season just a few weeks later.

In the interview clip these friends were discussing, Strahan asked Hamlin—by all accounts a young, healthy male with minimal risk factors—to talk about the cause of the incident.

"How did doctors describe what happened to you?" Strahan asked.

It seemed like a straightforward question.

Hamlin, however, hesitated.

"Um . . ." he said. And then, after another long pause, another "Um . . . ," finally, he responded: "That's something I want to stay away from."[17]

One of the people in the discussion immediately stated with complete confidence and without second thought the story he *knew* was true. Hamlin, he said, hesitated because the truth contradicted a certain accepted narrative regarding health requirements of the times and Hamlin was told not to mention it.

That *could* be the story. *But what else could it be?*

Another person in the group suggested that maybe a different "interested party" (hint: the NFL) was already under a lot of pressure regarding the dangerous nature of the game itself, and a one-in-a-million tackle could draw more unwanted scrutiny.

And yet another person in the group (they were on a roll now) wondered if the story could be that there were other factors Hamlin didn't want to divulge. After all, he had hesitated in the same way when asked a different, completely unrelated question. Could the story be that there were some aspects of the experience Hamlin wanted to keep private?

Or! Could it be he is a person who chooses his words carefully? Was there a story of when he'd been burned in the past by speaking too soon? Or! Was he still feeling shaken about the health event and didn't want to become emotional? Or! Editing?! Was the interview edited a particular way to fuel ratings for the network?

At the end of the "could it be" exercise, the group concluded that ultimately . . . there was no way of knowing. Because none of them *knew* Damar Hamlin. Any of the imagined storylines were just that—imagined with no evidence—and they'd probably *never* know what the true story was.

Which is also important to note.

Sometimes the story simply isn't yours to know—either because the person doesn't want to share it or you don't have the proverbial security clearance. In these cases, do not worry. Simply *knowing* that there's a story is better than knowing what the story *is*.

In this way, a Story Forward Leader can become a "story advocate." In moments when something doesn't seem to add up, the best leaders don't automatically fill in the empty void with the first, likely biased, story that comes to mind or that they intuit. A Story Forward Leader sees the first story as an *option* while looking for more stories that might reveal a deeper or more nuanced truth.

When asked about the importance of this kind of second-guessing, Sara Hodges, PhD, a professor of psychology at the University of Oregon, replied: "As scientists we second-guess our assumptions all the time, looking for alternative explanations . . . we need to do that as people too."[18] I would add: especially if you find yourself making a negative assumption—particularly about another person—pause and take a moment to second-guess.

MORE STORY = BETTER DECISIONS

Though it may be considered countercultural to take an extra beat, stay curious, and make your decisions more slowly, all signs point to the importance of leaders who are not just decisive but draw on the wisdom of the stories they seek.

Not only does knowing *there is always a story* improve your decision-making, it is also the pathway to another leadership trait that is not easy to teach: empathy.

The next chapter will help us with all the feels.

FIVE

Empathy 101

"When we share our stories,
we are reminded of the humanity in each other."
—MICHELLE OBAMA

It was a Tuesday morning in November. It was early. Too early. It was still dark outside and yet there I was, climbing endless flights of stairs in my bulky winter coat to reach the third-floor gymnasium of my daughter's elementary school to watch an early morning "Ultimate" tournament. Not to be confused with Ultimate Frisbee, Ultimate is like a mash-up of basketball (with no dribbling) and soccer (but you use your hands) and keep-away.

I walked into the gymnasium and quickly worked my way over to the bench where all the other bleary-eyed parents were sitting, among them a mom I hadn't seen before. She was groggy like the rest of us, but she still looked fabulous. It wasn't her clothing or that she had a lot of makeup on, but more like the glam was just permanently *there*. The lashes, the brows, the cheeks, the lips, and the hair that—even in a baseball cap and against all odds—screamed "Cool Mom."

Because I was a little late, the only place left to sit was next to a dad I knew who was talking to Cool Mom. Reliving my high school lunchroom nightmares, I walked up to the pair and asked if I could sit with them. They nodded.

We sat for forty-five minutes, me, the Cool Mom, and the dad in between us, chitchatting between plays, and I found myself really enjoying Cool Mom. She was sharp and sarcastic, and, if a little reserved at first, her manner evolved into a crispness I appreciated.

By the time the tournament was over, I was fully awake and said, perhaps too cheerily, "Remind me your name?" She told me. "Great. Nice to meet you. I'll see if I can find you and connect on Instagram or something." She nodded, smiled, and disappeared into the sea of parents ready to get on with the rest of the day.

As I left the gym, I ran into another mom. "Oh! I didn't even see you come in! Where were you sitting?" I mentioned Cool Mom. "Ohhhh . . . yeah . . . I've seen her around . . .," she said in a distinctive "judging a book by its cover" tone.

THE BOOK & COVER CONUNDRUM

It's important to note, that tone is not an anomaly. It's not unique to Upper East Side moms. It's not unique to women. This tone can be heard across countless interactions between women and men, including, but not limited to, casual conversations on the putting green, opening-night receptions at annual conferences, meetings in small boardrooms discussing members of teams from different divisions, and TGIF happy hours after a long week.

Though we know we are not supposed to judge a book by its cover, research shows we absolutely do. As human resources expert

Jenny Heyes puts it: "According to evolutionary psychology, 'judging a book by its cover' is an inherent human trait which dates back thousands of years and is a natural instinct based on survival."[1]

However, though snap judgments may be part of our biology, resisting nature's call to immediate judgment is essential to effective leadership and is as simple as remembering, especially when it comes to people: "There's a story there." Just as I learned later that afternoon after the Ultimate game, when I searched for Cool Mom on Instagram.

I'd never heard her name before but she popped up right away and, just as you might expect, all of her photos were stunning. Like she'd clipped them out of magazines and taped them into her feed. Wait . . . maybe she *was* a model?! I hadn't heard what she did for a living . . . and then, as I scrolled one more row, a photo stood out. It looked different from the rest.

It was of a woman, a girl in her mid-twenties maybe. The photo was from a while ago, you could tell by the fashion and the graininess of the image itself. The girl was crying. More than crying. She looked broken, shattered; she was beautiful, healthy, and completely devastated. In her hands was a piece of paper with two colored photos printed on it. One photo of a smiling young man, the other of the same young man with his arm lovingly draped around . . . her.

At the top of the sheet of paper it read: "Missing from 2 World Trade Center 104th fl."

Wait . . . what? I thought. I read the caption, parts of which I'll include here. It tells the story of a devastating loss Cool Mom had endured years before.

21 years ago I lost the love of my life, Andy O'Grady. He was a managing director at Sandler O'Neill on the 104th

floor of Tower 2. His was the second tower to be hit (at 9:03am) but the first to fall (at 9:59am). I was at work, Bloomberg TV, and we were of course covering the news.

I have so many memories that are just as vivid as if it was yesterday. I remember speaking to him and what he was saying on the phone. I remember watching his building fall and not being able to catch my breath. I remember the whole newsroom floor got silent. They had all just watched me watch Andy die.

This event changed who I was completely. I had searched for the man who was "my one" all my life, and had finally found him and we were planning our wedding, and then this tragedy.

I remember hearing that Andy might be at Bellevue Hospital on a list of people who made it out, so I ran over there. And this is where the iconic photo was taken of me searching for him.

It was the honor of my life to have been loved by James Andrew O'Grady. I am thankful that because of this photo, more people know his name. #myperson

The woman sitting on the bench next to me, Cool Mom, looked and, more important, *felt*, nothing like the girl in that photo. And Cool Mom knew it—she said it in her caption, her father-in-law-who-never-was would one day say it in an interview, and I could tell from a casual interaction on a Tuesday morning in an elementary school gym: she was a completely different person. And yes, there would be plenty of people who might assume things based on her Cool Mom vibe, but if they knew *that* story, might they at least feel a little more empathy?

The person I met that day was the living, breathing, ever-after of a *story*.

And she's not the only one.

Every single person you encounter is the result of their stories. Stories that shaped them, that changed them. No matter who they are or how well you *think* you know them . . . *there is always a story.*

Great leaders know that all books have a cover—it's part of how books are made; it protects the more delicate contents printed on the pages from the elements—but Story Forward Leaders actively resist the urge to judge the book by the cover and instead seek to understand the stories written on the pages inside.

ACCESS TO EMPATHY

Consistently ranked as one of *the most important requirements* of leaders today, we are officially in our "Empathy Era." Everyone from Tony Robbins to *Forbes* magazine to the Center for Creative Leadership (and countless more) insist that leaders need to address today's challenges creatively while also showing sincere empathy.

Empathy done right is heralded as a positive skill to practice in business. Research has tied empathy to innovation in times of crises, increased agility, boosting productivity, fostering inclusion, and much more. And while research has determined that how empathetic we are is partly due to genetics, variation by genes accounts for a mere 10 percent.[2] That leaves a full 90 percent of individual differences in empathy derived from non-genetic factors—which means, empathy is not a set trait. It is not predetermined at birth. Empathy can be practiced, learned, and cultivated.

That said, empathy isn't all sunshine and rainbows. Empathy can promote antagonism and favoritism and be a draining skill if not practiced correctly.[3] It can be written off as a trait of the weak—too soft, too emotional, not a fit for the harsh realities of the workplace. And yet I find the bad reputation comes mostly from a lack of clarity for what empathy really is and guidance on how to achieve it.

One definition describes empathy as "the skill of (1) connecting with others to identify and understand their thoughts, perspective, and emotions; and (2) demonstrating that understanding with intention, care, and concern."[4] And experts often point to two ways to demonstrate empathy. First, by thinking about someone else's thoughts (cognitive empathy), and second, by considering someone else's feelings (emotional empathy).[5]

Here's where things get a little confusing for me because, though I am no empathy expert, both of those approaches seem flawed. Don't they? Both center on the observer thinking about others' thoughts or feelings . . . but without *any actual input* from the "others" at all. How can true empathy be achieved if it only happens within the vacuum of the observer's own perception?!

Instead, let's use this approach published by the American Psychological Association:

"The foundation of empathy has to be a willingness to listen to other peoples' experiences and to believe that they're valid."[6]

There is always a story holds the key to how this "willingness" is activated every day. *There is always a story* is the antidote to our snap judgments and the subtle walls we build to keep "others" out. At any given time, you are just one story away from knowing, from understanding, from connecting with the people you lead.

HUMAN CONNECTION IN
ONE STORY FLAT!

Lakshmi Rengarajan is a leading voice in building modern workplace connections. Her unique perspective comes from a diverse background, ranging from working in the dating industry at Match.com to serving as WeWork's director of Workplace Connection. Currently she serves as a Community Design Consultant who helps major brands foster relationships among their employees and ultimately reach their collaborative potential.

In a recent interview on the popular podcast *Pivot,* Rengarajan shared how her work has shown, again and again, the importance of *delaying* judgment and how powerful hearing just one story can be.

As an example, she recalled a work meeting and a man she didn't notice at first. "He could have just been wallpaper," she admitted. And then he gave a presentation about sports marketing. "But it wasn't just about sports marketing . . . it was about his life and how he arrived at this moment," Rengarajan shared. As he told the endearing and important story, the man started to look *different* to her. She understood so much more about him, who he was, his motivation, his passions. Over the course of just twenty minutes and one small story, a person she hadn't even noticed before suddenly became . . . *human.*[7]

Now more than ever, people are craving connection in the workplace. They long to be understood and valued as their whole selves. A recent article in *Forbes* said that "simply feeling disconnected from their coworkers is a top reason employees would quit." On the flipside, the writer Mark C. Perna went on to say that employees who feel connected are not only more motivated but also more productive.[8]

Connections matter, but make no mistake—connection must start with *you*. The leader.

This is *your job*.

As the leader, or as the leader you aspire to be, it is up to *you* to seek out the stories in your organization. To provide opportunities for stories to be shared. If you want to acquire great talent, raise strong leaders, and help them reach their greatest potential, you must learn their stories. If you want to create an environment that not only *claims* to be diverse and inclusive but actually *is*—one that connects and understands and uses the power of diverse experience and thought—you must hear their stories. My hope is that you'll be excited for the stories you'll hear and inspired by the difference that learning and knowing those stories can make—especially when it comes to raising the next generations of leaders.

USE STORIES TO DEVELOP RISING STARS

A growing concern facing many organizations is the development of leaders. According to *Harvard Business Review* and many other publications and thought leaders, the need for leadership development has "never been more urgent."[9] And while many organizations have programs in place that pragmatically match mentor and mentee, over the years these developmental relationships have become "increasingly superficial, transactional, and ineffectual—if they even existed at all."[10]

Growing leaders today requires more than just providing opportunities for promotion or visibility, onboarding or instruction, or simply sending "You've got this!" notes of encouragement. The developmental relationship identified as most effective by Herminia Ibarra, a professor at the London Business School, and published in the November–December 2022 *Harvard Business Review*, was that of *authentic sponsorship*. In this relationship, both public advocacy (instruction, career advancement) *and* relational authenticity are essential.

How do you achieve relational authenticity? By developing a real relationship.

How do you develop a real relationship? By getting to know someone.

How do you get to know someone? By letting them share their stories.

One of the most challenging aspects of current leadership development is how *different* the rising leaders are from the ones who currently sit at the top. Those who currently hold most of the power don't necessarily "look like" the talent that is (or should be) rising through the ranks. There are generational divides, gender divides, cultural and social dissimilarities—all barriers that need to be crossed and overcome.

This is the reality. How you *feel* about this reality—or which divide you find yourself in, and on which side—is a discussion for a different time. Right now, as someone who wants to lead better (which you are or you wouldn't be reading this) and build stronger teams and, as a result, stronger organizations, the important thing to remember is this:

In the space between any perceived dissimilarities, there is a story.

And the more stories you know, the better you will be at guiding your people to their individual bests. For example, in one of the leadership development relationships studied and discussed in the aforementioned *HBR* article, a junior who felt daunted by being a mother of young children and wasn't sure if she could take on the responsibilities of the next level felt comfortable sharing that story with her senior. The senior, listening to this story, had a better understanding of her behaviors and motivation and was able to communicate to her that she *was* ready. "That vote of confidence . . . was exactly what I needed," the junior explained.[11]

On the contrary, another developmental relationship in the research did *not* lead to a junior moving up. Susana, the junior, and Jim, the senior, began their relationship by discussing Susana's ambitions. Jim made some email introductions and Susana was grateful, but the relationship quickly fizzled. According to Susana, the two simply didn't connect. Jim's approach was to share the inflection points in *his* career versus seeking to understand Susana's career better, which led to misaligned guidance. Eventually "their relationship stagnated."

While the reasons one mentor relationship succeeds and another does not are highly complex, taking the time to truly get to know the person you're guiding is a key factor to success. And yes, "juniors and seniors need to understand that they maybe have to invest a lot of time and energy in getting to know their partners before they'll discover what they have in common,"[12] and what stories they share. But the stories are where the deep similarities in values and beliefs live—and not just stories from their professional experience but from their lives outside of work as well. If you're looking to raise stronger teams, hearing those stories is worth the investment of time and effort. And here's one strategy for doing it.

STRATEGY #4:
ASK QUESTIONS THAT ADD DIMENSION

In a February 2023 *Pivot* podcast interview and in regard to her work in dating apps, Lakshmi Rengarajan mentioned the term *dimensionalized*. Especially in online dating, but also as we peruse job applications or consider who to promote, not to mention how much work still happens virtually, "We are all getting flattened by our screens." Quite literally. And as a result, Rengarajan, as well as many other experts in the field of empathy and those of us (or just me) in the field of storytelling, recommend *asking better questions*.

What makes a good question? Or if you've heard that "open-ended" questions work well, what does that even mean?

Here are a couple of tips and questions* you can ask in an effort to dimensionalize your up-and-coming stars.

1.
Beware of questions that imply judgment.

An important piece of seeking stories is to ask questions in such a way that the storyteller doesn't feel like they're being tricked or trapped. "Tell me about your family" is certainly an open-ended inquiry, but the word "family" can be a heavy one—and might put the person on the defensive (which is the *opposite* of what we're trying to achieve). Instead, if you'd like to know about their history and understand that part of the story of who they are today, Rengarajan

---

* Human Resources often does a lot of the work for you. Be sure to consult formal guidelines of questions that can and cannot be asked.

recommends trying this question: "What was one great thing about your upbringing?" This gives plenty of options for the storyteller to choose from.

2.

"Tell me about one of your proudest moments outside of work."

A few things to note about this approach. First, it's actually not a question but rather an inviting statement. By starting with "Tell me about," you're implying that you're looking for a story, not just a general response. Second, by using the word "moment," once again you are guiding their thought process toward a *story* versus a general response. Finally, "outside of work" will help expand their imagination to other areas of life, enabling you to get to know the whole person—while at the same time not boxing them in to a specific area they might not be willing to share.

Certainly you can never know *all* the stories that another person has lived, but the best leaders know there is value in learning a few of them. In an increasingly two-dimensional world, even 3D isn't good enough. If we allow the act of *seeing* someone in person to qualify as a quality interaction simply because so many of our interactions happen digitally, we're still missing the richness that is possible and the potential that is there.

INCLUSION & BELONGING

Whether we like it or not, humans are programmed for tribalism. We didn't overtake other species and rise to the top of the food chain as individuals—total dominance came because we competed for the top spot as a *group*. We like groups. We like others who are *like* us and, as a result, "We just don't feel as much empathy for those we see as 'other.'"[13]

And though a group of people working at the same company, or in the same division, or at the same branch might foster some of the positive camaraderie necessary for success, challenges with *individuals* being treated as "other" because of factors such as race, religion, ethnicity, or sexual orientation is a challenge that, if an organization isn't already addressing it, they should be.

An especially important goal for modern organizations is to improve *inclusion*: the degree to which members of a workforce feel welcomed and empowered to contribute.[14]

The argument for improved diversity, equity, and inclusion (DEI) dates back to the Civil Rights Movement of the 1960s, but the modern DEI movement was reborn and widely emphasized following a series of high-profile civil rights violations in 2020.[15] In recent years, efforts have led to progress in both political and social arenas; however, DEI advocates point out that there is more work to be done: despite recent progress, problems like the LGBTQ+ community continuing to face discrimination, Black leaders occupying just 0.8 percent of Fortune 500 CEO positions,[16] and gender-pay disparities continuing to be widespread—to name just a few—persist.

Though seeking and sharing stories has long been the way humans increase empathy and understanding, when it comes to belonging and inclusion in the workplace, as organizations strive to become more diverse and increase representation at all levels, a common dilemma has emerged for cultural minorities whose identities are not only different but often associated with lower status. The dilemma "involves determining whether to highlight their dissimilarities"[17] or if doing so will have a negative impact on how they are perceived in the workplace.

There is concern, and research to validate the concern, that telling stories that bring attention to the nuances of cultural background will ultimately backfire and, therefore, minority-group employees might be better off keeping those stories to themselves. It feels like a lose-lose situation.

However, to my excitement (and hopefully yours), the most recent findings suggest that "minority employees may be able to express valued aspects of their cultural identities while gaining—as opposed to jeopardizing—inclusion." In 2023, Rachel Arnett, assistant professor of Management at the Wharton School, published an article entitled "Uniting Through Difference: Rich Cultural-Identity Expression as a Conduit to Inclusion."

The operative word: *Rich*.

Previous investigation into sharing cultural-background stories "has typically focused on superficial approaches to highlighting one's cultural background, such as hairstyles and brief references to an identity."[18] However, these are surface-level expressions and are, by nature, unlikely to increase inclusiveness because this kind of approach "encourages categorization . . . and activates stereotypes and biases."

In contrast, *rich* cultural-identity expression—exchanges involving sharing intimate feelings, details and information, inner thoughts and views, and personal experiences that offer insight into culturally relevant aspects of one's inner self—does have an impact.

In other words: expressions that contain the components of a *story*.

To test this, Arnett conducted several experiments. In one, employees from different companies were chosen to participate and, based on identifying questions, placed into pairs. Participants then took turns answering eight get-to-know-you questions, each participant sharing their answer before moving on to the next question.

Participants randomly assigned to the control group answered small-talk questions like:

"What is the best restaurant you have been to in the last month? Tell your partner about it."

Participants randomly assigned to the rich cultural-identity expression condition answered questions like:

"What aspect of your cultural background (i.e., your family origins, nationality, race, ethnicity, or area where you grew up) is the greatest source of pride for you? Why?"

Inclusive behavior was measured by centering on three well-accepted, primary indicators of inclusion:

1. *Status Perception.* The extent to which the majority employee perceives a minority coworker as admirable and deserving of respect.

2. *Closeness.* The feeling of interconnectedness and bonding between the self and another person.

3. *Learning Potential.* The degree to which majority-group employees believe they can learn from a minority-group coworker.

The three experiments "found evidence of majority-group employees behaving *more*—not less—inclusively toward minority workers who engaged in rich cultural-identity expression, as opposed to small talk." Evidence that knowing there is always a story, and learning what those stories are, has some incredible benefits.

However, though the results were promising, they came with an important point of awareness. Specifically: seeking these stories should not, *cannot,* come at the expense of or cause harm to the minority-group employee. The researcher asserted:

> Minority-group employees should not feel forced to engage in such expressions to educate others, cultivate inclusion, or make diversity "work." Rich cultural-identity expression involves making oneself vulnerable through deep personal sharing, especially when discussing negative topics. Such vulnerability may make some minority employees uncomfortable.
>
> Additionally, trying to explain less-known aspects of one's identity has the potential to be psychologically taxing, especially when doing so for another's sake rather than a personal desire for authenticity. . . . Given that some individuals may feel like the costs outweigh the gains, it is important that rich cultural-identity expression is a voluntary decision rather than something minority employees feel forced to engage in at work.[19]

With that assertion in mind, a leader's self-awareness is critical. By nature, the leader is in a position of power and has a unique impact on the experience of inclusion. It is up to the leader to create a safe environment for these diverse, culturally rich stories to be shared, but in which no one feels obligated to have to do so. With that in mind, here is another Story Forward strategy to try.

STRATEGY #5:
CREATE SPACE

In February 2023, the founders of SoulCycle launched a new concept called Peoplehood. Yes, it's a workout. No, not for your body. Peoplehood is a workout for your empathy muscles. Participants attend, either in a studio or virtually, a sixty-minute session called a Gather, where they practice the skill of active listening. A Guide leads the group through a peer-to-peer structure of thematic dialogue designed to, according to a press release, "Spark self-awareness, change perspectives, and lead to 'Aha!' moments." No advice, no additional questions, absolutely no interruptions, not a verbal "yeah"' or "uh-huh" is allowed (though aggressive nodding is).

The monthly membership is $95.

In case you're wondering, I have not attended a Peoplehood session. I admit to having had mixed feelings when I heard about it (starting with the hefty price just to be listened to, and who *won't* be heard simply because they can't afford to be . . .). But one thing they have gotten right—they've created a *space* for stories to be shared and, as a result, allowed empathy to bloom. Story Forward Leaders should take note.

Because of our aforementioned obsession with "moving fast," we have "getting down to business" set as our default. We might think that there are only so many hours in the day and time spent on "chitchat" is time wasted. While certainly meaningless gossip or endless rehashing of decisions is not productive, meaningful story-sharing deserves its place on the agenda. Dedicated time and attention, sustained commitment, and prioritization are necessary if you ever stand a chance of hearing the stories you need.

The "office calendar" is a necessary evil, but the degree to which some high-performers commit to it is shocking. One boss scheduled everything from "drink water" to "eat something green." Some leaders used their calendars as a way to reduce stigma around certain issues, scheduling their therapy and mental health appointments with full organizational transparency. Another article detailed the embarrassing realizations some employees had when discovering their calendar was public to the organization instead of private. (Memorably, one man put an event on his calendar to remind him to pick up a rotisserie chicken for dinner. Then a colleague messaged him about a product meeting. "The only good spot for most people, you have a blocker called 'get a chicken,'" she wrote. "Is that something you could move to join us?")[20]

Yes, a calendar is a powerful tool for keeping your commitments and, conversely, if it's not on the calendar, it won't get done. I imagine you can see where this is going.

Pausing to consider that there is a story behind every perceived obstacle and being prepared with questions to unlock those stories won't do you any good if you don't have time *built into the workday* to allow this kind of communication to occur. Instead of perceiving story-sharing as mere chitchat or the thing you do before the "real stuff" starts, schedule story-sharing into recurring meetings as an agenda item. Even tuck it in the middle of the meeting, not as the first thing, forcing the team to switch gears.

One additional suggestion I always recommend, which happened to be seconded in the "Uniting Through Differences" article, is this: If you are seeking stories, then a leader should make themselves vulnerable through their own self-disclosure. It's a concept I call: Story Begets Story. As one person self-discloses, the recipient is likely to reciprocate. (Ah, but now I'm getting ahead of myself; we'll talk about *that* in the next section.)

Taking time and making an effort to understand the *stories* behind and within the people with whom we spend so much of our lives— let's face it, the *majority* of our time with—allows us to achieve the necessary fourth dimension that so many humans are craving.

MISS UNDERSTOOD

Before wrapping up this first part—that *there is always a story* and you and your business will be better if you take time to learn what it is—I'd like to go back, once more, to Cool Mom. Because as it turns out . . . there's more to *that* story too.

After my daughter's team's abysmal showing at the Ultimate tournament, I decided to sign her up for a dodgeball league (which included Cool Mom's daughter) to see if they could win for once. And that's exactly what they did: win once. One game at the very last dodgeball tournament.

Though the girls didn't win any championships, the season wasn't a total loss. The true winners included me and Cool Mom, who became better friends by getting to know each other's stories and the ups and downs of working, raising daughters, and everything else that comes with it. At the after-party following our last game, she mentioned that her brand-new podcast was just about to launch . . . a podcast called *Miss Understood.*

The description reads:

> This podcast delves into the lives of those who have been reduced to a single headline. Each episode will take a

closer look at the stories of those who are on a mission to change their narrative. Through raw and honest conversations, we will reveal the human behind the headline.

It turns out Cool Mom, based on her own experience and for better or worse, was a more-than-qualified host. While I only knew her as Rachel, the Cool Mom at Ultimate, and then as the woman whose photo of quintessential anguish went viral across the world in the days following 9/11, the rest of the country (and the world) probably knew her best as Rachel Uchitel . . . Tiger Woods's mistress. Well, one of them.

Maybe you recognize her name, maybe you only recognize his. Either way, within all of us are endless stories. Stories that shape who we are, how we show up, who we trust, who we don't, and why.

In all cases, when it comes to the people you work with (and all people in general, honestly), look beyond the proverbial headline and read the full story. It's the only path to empathy. I've said it before, and I'll say it again: *there is always a story.*

A STORY NEEDS TO BE TOLD

How to Influence and
Inspire Those You Lead

SIX

If You Want
Something Done . . . a
Story Must Be Told

"Stories have power . . .
Want to make a point or raise an issue? Tell a story."
—JANET LITHERLAND

I n 2019 Paul Mauger was asked to serve as interim director for a fire and emergency medical services department. The previous director had left, and based on Paul's stellar reputation serving in the capacity of chief of a neighboring county, the board knew he was the right man to run things while government leadership searched for a replacement.

Though Paul knew his time with the organization would be short, he also knew there were things that needed to get done. And, as his colleagues expressed, if Paul is anything, he's a "get things done" kind of guy. The first item on the agenda? Replacing the SCBA.

For those unfamiliar with expensive lifesaving equipment, SCBA stands for Self-Contained Breathing Apparatus, and it is extremely important when entering a lethal atmospheric environment. The SCBA at this organization had long passed its life expectancy and was in desperate need of replacement. Of course, as one might guess, it is no small financial feat to replace an SCBA, and often multiple units are required, depending on the size of the organization.

The former director had attempted, on three occasions, to present to county leaders on the need for this investment. To his credit, he was able to secure *some* funding appropriated for the initial purchase of the equipment. Unfortunately, no consideration was given to a long-range replacement plan.

Paul immediately got to work investigating the status and what would be required financially to see the installation through. "Based on my estimation," he told me, "we would need an additional $1.2 million." The only way to get this money was to stand before a boardroom of decision-makers, state his case, and ask for it the old-fashioned way.

"As is typical for most presenters, I fell into the trap of preparing PowerPoint slides inclusive of data," Paul said. At the end of his preparation, he had seven slides. "I referenced recognized fire services replacement standards and the age of the current apparatus. I detailed what the risks were if we *didn't* replace the equipment, as well as the cost and number of units needed, etc."

Then, the night before his presentation, it suddenly occurred to him that this was the wrong approach. The decision-makers didn't need more data—this was likely the exact data the previous guy had shared. If this were about logic and sense, they would have approved the project years ago—community members *die* without this equipment.

No, Paul realized that what his pitch needed was . . . a story.

"That night, with just hours before the presentation, I threw everything I had prepared away and started crafting my story."

And what a story it was.

Years prior, while serving in another organization, Paul responded to a hazardous-material incident where an unmarked tractor trailer on the roadside was leaking a milky white substance. First on the scene were two law enforcement officers. In an effort to see what was in the rear of the truck and better understand the situation, one of the officers pulled himself up onto the truck, took a deep breath, and suddenly realized there was a problem. His eyes started to water, his lungs burned, and mucus flowed uncontrollably from his nostrils.

When Paul arrived, he instructed the patrolman to strip down so that he could be decontaminated. Although he was reluctant to do so (as they were in the middle of a highway), the officer followed Paul's directive.

Paul didn't tell me, Kindra, what was in the truck that was so dangerous, only that sadly, the patrol officer suffered an extended loss of taste and smell, permanent liver damage, and partial lung damage. The patrol officer's supervisor, the other man on the scene, who had only walked within *proximity* of the truck, suffered permanent lung damage that contributed to his inability to return to work.

The attending physician stated that had emergency decontamination not been performed with equipment much like that which Paul was asking for from the board, most likely the officers would have died.

That was it. That is the story Paul Mauger would tell.

And the next night, he did.

Paul stood in front of the room, without his original slide deck, and shared this story with the decision-makers. He compared that incident with a potential incident in their jurisdiction where a citizen may be trapped in a house fire, but responders are unable to rescue them because of faulty or absent SCBAs.

The presentation was brief. Twenty minutes at most, including questions. And as he concluded, one board member openly stated, "Now *that's* how you make a request!"

Even the police chief, who was also at the meeting—public safety in any community always competes for the same bucket of money—congratulated Paul: "I sure am glad I don't have to follow that." Paul and his department were awarded $1.2 million to be put toward the long-term replacement plan and activation of the SBCA.

TRUTH 2:
A STORY NEEDS TO BE TOLD.

Paul Mauger's successful request for funding provides a powerful illustration of the second essential Truth that give leaders the Story Edge:

A story needs to be told.

Standing at the fork in the road, Paul took the path less traveled. Instead of merely sharing facts and figures as those before him had done, he instead knew that a *story needed to be told.* Only a story, something that has been at our disposal since the dawn of humankind, would connect with his audience and influence them *so* deeply that they would be not only willing but *compelled* to take the action he desired.

If the first Truth is *There is always a story* and you will be a better leader if you take a moment to figure out what it is, the second

Truth of Story Forward leadership is knowing that when the questions are big and the struggles are real, that is when *a story needs to be told.*

Whether a story is told by an executive on a podcast, a software developer at the vending machine, or a tired parent at their child's bedside, stories can offer inspiration, comfort, and ideas for taking action.

When it comes to influence and inspiration, storytelling is the original people mover. Like the moving walkway at an airport, once you step on and engage in the story being told, there really are no other options than to go in the direction you're going, in a straight line, and likely faster or at least with less effort than if you had walked the same distance without the story's help.

If you are struggling to get buy-in from your team, if your arguments fall flat and your reasoning doesn't get the job done—*a story needs to be told.* If you're looking to bolster creativity, motivation, productivity—*a story needs to be told.* If you're struggling to get the right people on board or keep the people you have—*a story needs to be told.*

If you are struggling to connect or build trust or make an impact or inspire action, it means you aren't telling a story . . . even if you think you *are* telling one, which is a problem worth discussing.

THE STORY THAT WASN'T

I'm what you might call a "multiple-planner planner." I have a calendar on my phone, another one on my computer, one in a journal that is more behavior-tracking than daily-meetings based, and finally, a spiral-bound day planner.

The day planner is by far the bulkiest of all my planners because, per the title "Daily Planner," it has an entire page dedicated to every day of the year *plus* a monthly view and a few additional pages that address topics including dreams and goals.

The creators of this planner were clearly trying to make *more* than just a "planner." It includes stickers, the aforementioned "dreams and goals" section, *and,* according to the title on one page . . . a *story.*

Printed on one of the first pages of the planner in big, bold letters it reads:

THE STORY of the Planner that will Change Your Life

I'll abbreviate the content that follows that rousing header here:

> At Day Designer® we believe that everyone can design— and live a life that they love, and our mission is to help you do just that.
>
> Day Designer products combine beautiful designs, helpful content, and easy-to-use planning pages that inspire and guide users to find balance, focus, and productivity.
>
> Day Designer was born in 2010 to help people live better, with less stress. A quick sketch that combined a to-do list, schedule, notes, and gratitude became the trademarked Today & To-Do® page design at the heart of every Day Designer. . . .
>
> We invite you to open this Day Designer planner and begin to live more productively and joyfully in the coming year. Manage your time better and make each day

count—enjoying all the love, laughter, and adventure life has to offer.

Now, does that sound like a *story* to you?

Imagine inviting a friend out after work with this text: "Meet up after work? Have I got a story for you!" And then, over a glass of champagne or beer or whatever, you retold the Day Designer "story" above.

What do you think your friend would say? If they're nice, they'd probably just nod and change the subject. If they were honest they'd probably say, "I came all the way uptown for *that*?!" Or if your kids asked for a bedtime story and you read to them from the Day Designer, what would happen? The only possible benefit is that they'd be asleep before they could complain. There is absolutely nothing in the essay above that is worth staying awake for.

When a tab on a company website reads "Our Story," or the second slide in a pitch deck says "The Story," or you start new-employee orientation with the statement "It's important that you understand our *story* . . . ," rest assured, none of these "promises of a story" guarantee that what follows will constitute an actual story.

Therein lies the problem. The reason so many people fail to fully access the Story Edge is because they think they already are.

To be clear, I don't blame the planner company for this gaffe because, well, they just don't know any better. *No one* seems to know better, because the skill of storytelling and what makes a story great isn't really taught. The Day Designer folks no doubt thought putting "The Story" at the top of the page meant that anything else that followed *was* a story. Most brands and companies do. Calling something a story seems to be the going standard for storytelling in leadership and business, and that's fine for the other guys, but now that you're here, reading this, I hope you will deem this sloppy excuse for a story no longer acceptable. Especially after I equip you with two things necessary to set Truth 2 in motion: Time and Technique.

TAKING THE TIME FOR THE STORY

Let's face it. In the grand scheme of message preparation, storytelling is an afterthought. We spend our time on the arguments, reasons, logic. We invest endless energy into font types and sizes. Many companies have entire teams dedicated to creating decks and briefings . . . but have you ever heard of a person whose entire job it is to find and carefully craft compelling stories? To match the information of the message to a story that will make it matter? Probably not.

I liken the neglect when it comes to telling good stories to the health recommendations about our diets. That is, you've likely heard that eating lots of cheeseburgers is not ideal for a person's health. The sodium, saturated fat, additives, cholesterol, refined carbohydrates . . . none of it is great for us.

However, eating *one* cheeseburger isn't going to lead to our immediate demise. And, especially if there's nothing else in the house to eat, ordering a cheeseburger and a nice salty side of fries can feel like the easiest and best answer to tackling your hunger.

Now, if greasy cheeseburgers *did* lead to our immediate demise, people would be much less likely to eat them. But eat them we do, and for some, they are a regular part of a diet that is slowly and incrementally destroying good health.

So, similarly, while it's true that *not* telling a story won't lead to your *immediate* demise, it will make you a little worse, a little bit at a time, and eventually, it'll all add up and you'll wonder why your team turns over so much, why your colleague got promoted over you, why you find it so hard to get people motivated or to care.

All the power that is available with the Story Edge is only accessible through, you guessed it, effort. Intention. Planning ahead. Now, as you master this skill, as you become *more* Story Forward naturally, telling the right story at the right time will come more easily.

But if you are at the beginning of that journey, here are the steps required to Tell the Story. Make a little bit of time for these and you'll notice a big change.

FOUR STEPS TO TELLING THE STORY

STEP ONE: *Clarify the Problem.* What is the obstacle? Where is the gap? What isn't working or what needs to work better? What are you trying to achieve and can't quite make happen? And don't forget: there is always a story.

STEP TWO: *Identify Your Objective.* What do you want your audience or listener to think, feel, know, or do once they've heard the story you tell?

STEP THREE: *Consider the Audience.* What do *they* care about? What are their interests? What is on their minds? What are they hopeful for or working toward?

STEP FOUR: *Find a Story at the Intersection of Steps One– Three.* Step Four is the hard part. Step Four takes the most work and practice, but once you see the stories in action, the effort is worth it.

Here's an example of how this method could be used to handle a workplace challenge.

Rebekah is the SVP of a large team responsible for the private equity arm of a substantial financial establishment. For the past ten years, Arday has been the VP of the division and reports directly to Rebekah. And though they've been working together for a decade, the two of them have never really meshed well. Arday, despite his esteemed role, often acted immaturely. He would throw adult-fits when asked to do something he didn't want to do, and he promoted people based on personal preference versus clearly stated company objectives. Ultimately, Rebekah believed Arday wanted to be promoted to *her* position, which simply wasn't going to happen.

Rebekah had tried to find ways to make their working relationship better, including, most recently, creating an entirely *new role* for Arday that was perfectly suited to his strengths and allowed him to build and hire his own team. For ten months, this arrangement seemed to be working, but then, out of the blue, Arday announced that for undisclosed personal and professional reasons, he was leaving the company.

Rebekah was shocked and frustrated and left in the lurch because now, in addition to all of the quotas she was personally responsible for, she also had an entirely new team to manage—a team that broke down in tears when Arday told them he was leaving. From the response, one might think they'd lost a great leader in Arday . . . but a closer look revealed something much different.

It didn't take long to figure out that Arday's questionable work ethic had also infected the team, and all of Rebekah's concerns and suspicions were confirmed when she met with each member one-on-one. They each revealed various dysfunctions—people who couldn't do the job they *had* but were promised a promotion by

Arday. People who weren't held to the same production standards as someone else on the team in the same role. The list went on. Beneath the happy façade, animosity within the team was brewing.

Morale was low and the team, feeling as though they had just endured a crisis, was on the brink of collapse. Not to mention all of this happened right before Rebekah was slated to go on a global tour selling a new product to some of the highest–net worth people in the world. Rebekah had one chance, one all-team meeting scheduled to get everyone on the same page or lose the team all together.

Now let's take a moment to revisit the steps to help guide Rebekah as she seeks to save this sinking ship of a team:

Step One: Clarify the Problem. Low morale on a team that lost their (albeit dysfunctional) leader Arday and that is now reeling with uncertainty.

Step Two: Identify Your Objective. To help them understand that yes, things won't be the same, but in time, they can get even better.

Step Three: Consider the Audience. The team is mostly concerned about maintaining their individual levels of notoriety and perceived status within the organization.

Step Four: Find a Story at the Intersection of Steps One–Three. The intersection of the three things—the problem, the objective, the audience—will require a story that acknowledges the pain of uncertainty, the importance of fixing a thing that's broken so that it can be even better, and the possibility of maintaining reputation through it all. Additionally, the story should reveal some things about Rebekah so they can get to know, like, and trust her better as their new leader.

That being determined, there are several places Rebekah can look in her life, both personally and professionally, that might yield the perfect story. Such as:

- A time early in her career when things took a sudden turn and what she thought would be a setback actually led to a step up.

- The time she helped a friend who had lost her husband, and as they were trying to make sense of the records and accounts he kept, they realized it wasn't neat and tidy. He had some bad habits and problematic approaches, but with Rebekah's help, her friend was able to get through to the other side and is doing great. And with the same kind of dedication, this team can do the same.

The more detailed you get answering those first three questions, the better you will be at identifying a story that hits on those needs. And as you can see in this example, two viable options came to mind immediately. Certainly, there are many more. Each possible story will likely inspire *another* possible story. The key here is to give yourself enough time and thought space to find the story that needs to be told.

Now that you know to take the time to prepare a story and what to do with the time once you take it, let's talk technique. What does it take to tell a great story, and what makes a story great?

HOW TO CRAFT COMPELLING STORIES

My first book, *Stories That Stick: How Storytelling Can Captivate Customers, Influence Audiences, and Transform Your Business*, was published in the fall of 2019. I'm proud to say it was on nearly every bestseller list, including ranking number two by the *Wall Street*

Journal behind a book by Disney CEO Bob Iger. And while the epic ranking and bestseller status during launch week was thrilling, what matters more to me is that the book continues to be bought, read, and shared. It's sold hundreds of thousands of copies, is translated into fifteen languages, and continues to rank among the top books in business, sales, and selling.

I believe the reason for that book's success is not only my own authentic passion for storytelling but also because I wanted the "art" of storytelling to be more about the science. I wanted to provide a *blueprint* and a *practical system* for using stories in business.

In case you missed *Stories That Stick,* let me give you a super-brief overview of the simple storytelling framework, and the four key components that make stories more compelling, influential, attention-grabbing, and memorable.

The most widely known and taught way to craft a story is often referred to as "the three-act structure." Where a story is simplified into three parts: a beginning, a middle, and an end. But there is a more descriptive way to approach the framework; I choose instead to look at stories as *normal, explosion,* and *new normal.*

To tell a good story, first you have to make the audience care. To do this, you must establish the *normal*: the way that things were before they changed. Creating the normal allows the audience to recognize themselves within the story, which leads them to let down their guards and invest in the story. It lets them see parts of their own world within the story. When you skip the "normal" and jump into the middle of a story, the audience won't have the same connection to it. That's why, for example, we can watch the evening news without being emotionally invested: news stories jump right into the action. We see a burning apartment building, but not the calm scene of one of its residents unpacking her groceries the day before. The normal is the most important part of the story, and it's also the part that most people leave out.

Next is the *explosion*. The explosion, despite the word's admittedly aggressive connotation, is simply the happening: it's the moment when things change. Big or small, good or bad, the explosion is the point in the story when we leave the normal behind and enter a new, different reality.

The final part of the story is the *new normal*, where you enlighten your audience on what life is like now, post-explosion, after things changed. Maybe you've learned something, or maybe you're inspired to work toward something new. The new normal can demonstrate the moral of the story or include a call to action. Whatever the new normal is for your story, it is what makes a story work as a *strategy* in business instead of just as a means for entertainment.

Woven within these three phases are four components that work together to build effective stories: identifiable characters, authentic emotion, a moment, and specific details.

We'll start with the *identifiable characters*. Put simply, this is someone we connect to and understand—an individual we can identify and identify *with*. It cannot be a *group* of people (such as "our customers"), a company name, or a product.

Next is *authentic emotion*. This doesn't necessarily have to be a dramatic emotion, but it needs to be a feeling that is experienced by the characters or exists inherently within the story. This is important because, through that emotion, the story's readers or audiences can empathize with the story.

The third component to an effective story is a particular *moment*. This is the specific point in space, time, or circumstance that distinguishes the story from our everyday lives. The moment allows us to zoom in on the experience of the story rather than providing a vague, general description of an event, which is much less memorable.

Finally, the last component of a great story is *specific details*. This component involves the use of imagery and descriptive (sometimes unexpected) details that are relevant to the intended audience. These details can draw the audience in, allowing them to enter a world that feels familiar to their own. For example, if you're telling a story to an audience of parents, you might describe wrestling a stroller into the trunk of your car or a particularly deafening temper tantrum your toddler had at a grocery store. To connect with Gen X, you might reference a boom box or an Atari game system or the TV show *Saved by the Bell*. This final component is crucial, and the stickiest stories use specific details like these to build bridges between the storyteller and the audience.

To further validate these components, my team and I conducted a research study. We surveyed more than fifteen hundred parents about marketing copy written for a children's toy. We created two messages, one generic and one storied. Respondents were asked how compelling they found the marketing copy. In the storied copy, some text included all four great components of story (identifiable characters, authentic emotion, a significant moment, and specific details), some included three, some two, and some only one component. Our results were overwhelming; in all cases, the respondents preferred the storied copy to the generic copy, even if the copy only included one of the components. The storied copy, they said, was more compelling, more entertaining, more memorable, more persuasive, and more captivating. (Success!)

WHEN IN DOUBT, TELL THE STORY

It's true: when it comes to storytelling, I just can't help myself. It drives me a little mad to see a missed story opportunity, which is why after reading—and being so frustrated by—my daily planner's sad excuse for a story, I started imagining alternative options for the *actual* stories they could have told.

I imagined a woman like me purchasing the planner in a desperate haze—a woman whose life felt like it was speeding past in a blur. Even though she *knew* she had things to be grateful for, it was hard to keep track of them on her phone. Like me, it would help her to grow in gratitude if she would write things down and see them in her own handwriting in order to really work them out.

I imagined the pieces of my *own* story with the planner. How my briefcase was already *so heavy* with newspaper clippings (you know I love them) and research articles, and drafts and notes as I worked on the book that I was convinced that my right trapezius was permanently damaged from carrying it and yet, there I was, hauling the ten-pound planner around with me up and down subway stairs, through airports, and on the Long Island Rail Road because the planner made me feel less stressed about what I was doing (or not doing) and more connected to who I was becoming. The planner had become such a part of my daily life that it didn't matter how heavy it was; leaving it behind felt like I was abandoning a piece of myself. (Isn't that a more interesting story?)

Unable to let it go, I actually *found* the woman who had originally created the planner. Her name is Whitney English, and do you know what?

The first versions of the planner *did* tell her story.

It was the story of a woman who, in quick succession, had experienced explosive business success, had suffered a massive business failure, filed for bankruptcy, become a mother, and completely lost herself. Whitney told the story of wanting a place to plan the next version of her life and, not being able to find a planner up to the task, she created her own. She told her story on her blog, on socials, and in the planner itself as she began selling it, and eventually the planner *sold out* in Target . . . all because of her story.

Eventually, Whitney *sold* the planner for a hefty sum—and *that* was the planner I had.

The planner *without* her name on it.

The planner made possible by a story.

The planner that, according to Whitney, didn't *tell* the story anymore because that was the one piece of intellectual property she wanted to keep for herself. (And I can't say I blame her.)

The ability to influence and inspire is perhaps the most important aspect of truly legendary leaders. For those who embrace and embody and *believe* that, indeed, a story must be told, just as Fire Chief Paul Mauger did, they will be the ones who make things happen, who get things done.

The next two chapters will show you how.

SEVEN

The Ultimate
Influence Equation

$$\times$$

"Behind a life of influence
you will find a masterful storyteller."
—MOLLIE MARTI

V ietnam was in trouble.

Noncommunicable diseases (NCD) were on the rise, with a 30 percent increase in NCD mortality and morbidity in Vietnam between 1976 and 2009.[1] While the traditional Vietnamese diet is considered healthy, rapid urbanization and the changes that come with it led to increased intake of animal products, fats, and oils and a decreased intake of vegetables. This, combined with a shift from high-calorie-expenditure work (like manual labor and agriculture work) to urban desk jobs, contributed to increased struggles with obesity within the population.[2] To make matters worse, only one-third of individuals diagnosed in one area were even aware of their condition, and of those diagnosed with hypertension, only 43 percent were treated despite inexpensive health care and the fact that generic medications were readily available.[3]

Something needed to be done. Behaviors *had* to change but this was proving very difficult, especially in the more rural areas of the country. Previous health announcement strategies weren't moving the needle. The country was desperate for a new approach—a plan for novel, large-scale, and sustainable interventions to improve hypertension control.[4]

Researchers were determined to find it. And, already aware of the power of storytelling to influence behavior change, they decided to test the power of a storytelling intervention versus the traditional, didactic, information-based intervention to see if *story* might be the solution.

The researchers crafted two different intervention types to be administered to residents of several rural communities in northern Vietnam.

The storytelling intervention centered on patient stories about living with hypertension.

One group was given a DVD that included "general recommendations for managing several important risk factors for hypertension . . . including the importance of having a healthy diet, quitting smoking tobacco, drinking less or no alcohol, participation in regular physical exercise, and having regular examination checkups."[5]

The other group received a DVD that centered on culturally relevant stories in which patients told their own stories about how they were able to manage their hypertension effectively. They shared stories about family support or the challenges they faced when adjusting their lifestyle and what method they used—medication or otherwise—to manage their blood pressure.

The good news? Both groups benefited from the interventions. Blood pressure was reduced by 5.8mmHg in the didactic group.

The *better* news? Blood pressure declined by 10.8mmHg in the storytelling group—nearly double that of the control group.

Not only that, but "the storytelling group also experienced more improvement in several health behaviors, including increased levels of physical activity and reduced consumption of salt and alcohol."

The stories of other people's experiences dramatically influenced the behavior of those who heard the stories. More compelling than simple facts or reason, it was the stories that created overwhelming action and enabled dramatic, sustainable improvement in the patients' lives.

This is the kind of difference stories can make for *you* and *your* impact on behavior. If there is action you want from your team or behavior you want to instill, why would you ever settle for the didactic version—the one where you give a list of facts—when you *know*, it's *telling the story* that makes it happen.

Yes, telling a story takes more time—like the painstaking effort those researchers put in to not only find people to tell their stories but to film them and curate the most effective ones—and is a lot more work than the didactic alternative with its reliance on dependable facts and figures. But with more effort comes more reward.

Those who can move the masses, affect change and behavior, are those who use story to influence.

Which begs the question: What is *influence* anyway?

WHAT IS INFLUENCE, REALLY?

I feel a little bad for that word, "influence."

I mean, things were always a little dicey for it, right? Influence was always going to be vulnerable to the whims of connotation, but with the rise of the "Influencers" and their increasingly obnoxious antics (@influencersinthewild, anyone?), for a person to aspire to have influence might be taken as an aspiration to have a personalized code link for a skincare line or a horde of overenthusiastic followers (and equally enthusiastic haters).

However unsavory you might find "influencer culture," to have true *influence* is still powerful, admirable, and necessary if one hopes to thrive in business. I initially addressed the relationship between influence and storytelling in *Stories That Stick* (where the word "influence" is *in* the subtitle). And influence comes in a variety of shapes and forms. There are "hard" influence tactics and "soft" ones.[6] Varun Nagaraj and Jeff Frey, in a *Psychology Today* article, identified three types of influence that range from ethical to unethical.

1. Persuasion: Ethical influence, an appeal to self-interest via incentives. The follower has the ability to say "no."

2. Manipulation: Can be ethical or unethical influence; this includes hiding information or deceiving followers. It often uses a follower's emotions or fears to drive action. However, sometimes the ethics are tricky, such as in situations when the action must be taken for the follower's own well-being.

THE ULTIMATE INFLUENCE EQUATION

3. Coercion: Unethical influence, when the offer cannot be refused. This often includes a negative incentive (i.e., the follower must cooperate or else they'll lose their job).[7]

Most interesting, however, was a graph that detailed the effectiveness of nine different influence approaches. The ones that scored "most effective" were those that also required a high level of personal trust. One study found "inspirational appeals" the most effective, followed by consultation and personal appeals—all of which require a relationship and trust between the influencer and those being influenced.[8]

For a leader to lead effectively, followers *must* have trust on a variety of levels, including trust in the leader's intentions and abilities. They must trust that the leader has the best interests of the team and the company's shared goals at heart.

How do you build trust? The love songs might tell you that it takes time . . . which, yes, it can. But trust can also happen quickly with the right approach.

WHAT DO YOU NEED ON THIS JOURNEY?

On Sunday, January 8, 2023, Gary Burnison sent an email. Burnison, whom I mentioned in an earlier chapter, is the author of two books on career and effective leadership in the modern workplace. For nearly two decades he served as the celebrated CEO of Korn Ferry, a global organizational consulting firm specializing in solving a broad range of business challenges, from talent acquisition to leadership development and organization strategy.

In his email, he asked readers to imagine they were about to embark on a journey: a cross-country trip, on foot, leading ten thousand people from New York City to Santa Monica, California. Burnison mused:

> As you stand in Battery Park, at the southernmost tip of Manhattan, gathered around you are people from dozens of countries—different backgrounds, experiences, and perspectives. And your job is to lead this diverse group . . .
>
> We know that a solitary walker, putting in 10 hours a day, could cover those 2,800 miles in about 90 days. But this is not a race—it's about helping 10,000 people become more than they thought possible. Putting in about 2.5 hours a day, it will take our group a year—all of 2023.
>
> So, what do we need to take on this journey known as 2023?[9]

It was a fair question, asked by a worthy expert.

In his brief message that January, Burnison asserted that one of the essential items the journey would require was authenticity and transparent communication. Burnison is not alone. Research has shown employees' perception of leaders' authenticity to be the number one predictor of employee job satisfaction.[10] And transparent communication is positively associated with employees' trust in their organization.[11]

It's likely you yourself have proclaimed the importance of or insisted on a commitment to these qualities. However, as with most business buzzwords, talking about them is one thing. Embodying them, practicing them, and *being* authentic and transparent is another. Fortunately, every time you remember *a story needs to be told,* it's like a mile of city street with no traffic and all green lights. Here is the equation.

$$\text{INFLUENCE} =$$
$$(\text{AUTHENTICITY} + \text{TRANSPARENCY}) \times \text{TIME}$$

Your stories are the fastest, most effective way for your team to understand your feelings and commitment to the task at hand. Your stories are the best way for your team to believe you are up to the challenge. The stories a leader tells about their life, their experiences—their life stories—are perhaps the most legitimate and convincing means by which leaders can convey their commitment and credibility, "more legitimate and convincing than directly declaring their traits, values, and convictions."[12]

Finally, by telling your own stories you activate what is known as "disclosure reciprocity" (the scientific name for the aforementioned Story Begets Story), whereby the best predictor of how much one person will share is the level at which the other person initiated the interaction. "One way to gain information (or inputs) from others is to give them information about yourself first."[13]

If you are a leader who has hesitated telling your stories, this is your sign. Your team needs to know your stories. *You* need your team to know your stories both so they can connect with you *and* so they feel comfortable sharing their own.

Now, more than ever, people are skeptical. If you want your followers (employees, colleagues, acquaintances) to trust and feel connected to you as a leader—requirements for inspiring action and overcoming apathy—you must also tell *your* stories. The rest of the chapter will offer you insights and strategies you can use to access influence and trust through authentic, transparent communication . . . aka, when in doubt, *a story needs to be told.*

THE AGE OF AUTHENTICITY

Is it just me, or was there a time when the word *authentic* was mainly used in the context of or relating to leather? ("Our craftspeople create authentic, full-grain leather belts and bags you'll be proud to call your own!") Now, as Burnison stated in his email regarding what is required for success in the future, authenticity is an essential item for business success and survival.

According to the Harvard Business School, authentic leadership is "exhibited by individuals who have high standards of integrity, take responsibility for their actions, and make decisions based on principle rather than short-term success. They use their inner compasses to guide their daily actions, which enables them to earn the trust of their employees, peers, and shareholders—creating approachable work environments and boosting team performance."[14]

Watch the top leaders in any high-performing organization. The best of the best know there is no better way to build trust and influence with a team than through sharing stories. And it starts with their own.

NEW TEAM, OLD STORIES

It was a new day at Dell Technologies. After a recent reorganization, Rae, VP of the Southeast region, received the news that she would be assuming the responsibility of two new teams and with them, two new team leaders.

"While they are work relationships, they can also become very personal," Rae explained to me. One of the leaders who would now be reporting to Rae had previously had the same boss for fifteen years. "He had seen her through losing her husband, battling illness, and all the other ups and downs. In some ways, her old boss was the most consistent thing about her life . . . so to suddenly have that change, and to have a new person with a different management style . . . it's by nature a challenging situation."

Rae took over the new team at the beginning of the fiscal year. "We needed to get started quickly and effectively." However, she didn't live near either one of the new team leaders. "I could not go to them immediately and spend one-on-one time together." Both timing and distance meant she couldn't take them each out to dinner or an activity to get to know them face-to-face. "I had to find other ways for them to get to know me, to feel like they could trust me, to understand who I am, where I come from, and what I want from my career so they know why I'm doing what I do and why I may ask them to do things a certain way."

Rae's strategy: Telling stories. Lots of different kinds of stories.

"I wanted to find as many ways for them to connect to me as possible." To this end, Rae not only shared stories about really great wins in her career, but also about really big mistakes. She shared stories about her experiences in the workplace, and about her personal life. "I would start out calls by telling them a funny story about my kids, so they could see and feel that part of my life, too."

I'd like to pause for a moment and draw your attention to the paragraph above. If your goal is to build trust to enable healthy influence, then it is in your best interest to share the stories of the *many* different aspects of who you are. Do not fall into the trap that limits your stories to "customer successes" or "professional experience." While there is a place for those stories, your goal is to increase the surface area of possible connection, and story variety is the best way to do it.

For Rae, the storytelling was working. Her new team was able to understand quickly how and why she handled meetings with clients the way she did, why she didn't micromanage a team the way other managers did (which some team members preferred!). And perhaps most important, when it came to the single most important question her new team was privately asking themselves:

Will Rae have my back the way my old manager did?

Rae had a story for that too . . .

Except—this one came with a twist (and let me tell you, this is some advanced Story Forward work right here and—*wow!*—is it impressive). In addition to the stories *she* told, there was a story she didn't see coming.

"I recently visited the two districts that I took over and had one of my account reps travel with me. Initially it was so he could share his experience with some tools and processes he uses that I'd like the division to start implementing, but then I realized there was something more powerful happening. Throughout the trip people were constantly asking him what I was like, and how it was working for me. They were nervous, I get it. But what I wasn't expecting was when they asked, he told them *our* story. The story of how he and I started working together."

The story was a powerful one. Rae had made a huge difference in the rep's life in a very challenging time. When it looked like his future with the company was over, Rae had his back, advocated for

THE ULTIMATE INFLUENCE EQUATION

him, and managed to make a potentially devastating situation survivable. Each time he told the story, he ended it by saying, "You all hit the lottery with her. You may question what she asks you to do, but know that she always has your best interest at heart, and there's no one else I'd want in my corner."

That single story made everything a whole lot easier, and today, Rae is happy about the way things are developing with the new leaders and team. "The relationships are growing—they're new and different and it's exciting."

Yes, telling stories can lead to authentic leadership. The question you might now be asking is—how? How and where do I start? Well . . . let's start with *you*.

STRATEGY #1:
DEVELOP A DISCIPLINE OF
REVISITING YOUR LIFE STORIES

We're usually so busy living (or more accurately managing and surviving) the particulars and minutiae of our *current* life stories that we don't often look back and consider the *lifetime of stories* that have shaped us up until this point.

Stories of the people and events that shaped your childhood.

Stories of trouble you got into and why.

Stories of big choices you made—and whether or not you knew at the time how big they were.

Stories of heartbreaks and failures.

Stories of subtle triumphs.

How did you spend your summer? Where did you sit in the lunchroom? When was the first time you felt out of place and what happened? How did you meet your first best friend and are you *still* friends? Why or why not?

It might seem like a waste of time, all this backtracking down memory lane—especially since none of the examples I just listed ask about your resume or business experience. However, researchers have expressed that exploring the full richness of the stories a leader has lived provides necessary "knowledge and clarity about their values and convictions."[15]

In a 2005 article published in *The Leadership Quarterly*, "What's your story? A life-stories approach to authentic leadership development," researchers acknowledged that while leaders who are authentic and committed to their values and convictions are essential to true and lasting success in business, sometimes "authentic" is hard to achieve because we don't have the necessary clarity when it comes to our own values and convictions. With so many competing interests and so much noise, it can be difficult to even *find* our "inner compass," much less follow it. How can a leader be sure what they believe is *truly* what they believe and is not influenced by the unrelenting pressures of the environment? The solution, according to the researchers:

"Here, we suggest that leaders acquire these characteristics by constructing, developing, and revising their life-stories. Life-stories can provide leaders with a 'meaning system' from which they can act authentically . . . interpret reality and act in a way that gives their interpretations and actions a personal meaning. Therefore, leaders are authentic to the extent that they act and justify their actions on the basis of the meaning system provided by their life-stories."[16]

In other words: if you want to truly *be* authentic instead of *trying* to be authentic, take a moment and explore your own life stories.

Here are a few more prompts to get you started:

- What was the biggest decision you ever made—how did it turn out?

- Was there a particularly challenging time where you had to make a difficult choice?

- Was there a time when things didn't turn out the way you expected, and how did you handle it?

- What are the moments in your life of which you are the proudest?

- Who are the people who have influenced you, and how?

- Of all the places you have lived, where have you most felt at home?

- When did you feel most celebrated? Most humbled?

The good news is, when it comes to your life stories, there are no wrong answers and no restrictions. The stories don't have to come only from your professional experience or even from your adulthood. Nor do the stories have to necessarily be "associated with the overcoming of difficulties or hardships . . . there is considerable potential for leadership development in positive life events."[17] Any story that offers insight into the essence of who you are and what you know to be true is valuable; it is a story that can be told to others so that they fully understand that essence too.

In addition to your "life stories" that illustrate your authenticity, here are a few other types of stories to help pave the way to influence by building trust.

TELL STORIES WHEN THINGS FALL APART TO BECOME MORE TRANSPARENT

Transparency is a viable strategy in turbulent times, even when one's instinct might be to go into full-on Watergate, Pentagon Papers, tobacco industry cover-up mode. You know: denials, half-truths, claims of amnesia, bribes, and all manner of shady tactics.

But research tells us: "Employees who believe their employer communicates transparently show markedly higher scores for employee experience and engagement" and those "employees who perceive their *companies* to be transparent have 12x greater job satisfaction than employees who have the opposite perception."[18]

The reality is that things go wrong. Leaders make the wrong decisions and have to recover. When these things happen, tell the story. Tell the story of how and why something unpredictable, unpleasant, or ill-fated has happened. If there are parts of the story or details that you have to leave out to protect the innocent or for legal reasons, be honest and disclose that you can't tell the entire story. But tell as much as you can! *A story needs to be told* makes transparency, and all the good that can come of it, possible. Just ask Graza and its CEO, Andrew Benin.

Graza olive oil is a high-quality product that, unlike other olive oils of similar caliber, is affordable enough that people can actually *cook* with it instead of "save it" for when the Queen comes over and you serve it on the special china with an heirloom tomato or two. Let's face it, the Queen (may she rest in peace) is definitely not coming now, and to make actually *using* the delicious, well-priced Graza olive oil even easier, it comes in a convenient squeeze bottle.

Graza is basically the olive oil the world has always needed but didn't know it and, once it discovered it, the world needed it . . . *now*. That meant the 2022 holiday season, the first for the delicious start-up, was poised to be an exciting one. According to the *Wall Street Journal*, Graza's Sizzle & Drizzle cooking oil/finishing oil combo was featured in hundreds of gift guides, and demand was off the charts.

In fact, it was so far off the charts that the pressure squeezed the start-up until it all but imploded. Gift sets were not sets, as advertised, but just individual bottles in a box. Bottles arrived dented. Even the embossing on the logo flaked off. Sure, it was unlikely anyone was gifting Graza to the Queen, but still, it was a disaster, and CEO Benin knew it. And instead of hiding from it, he sent an email that told the story.

"Hello, very important Graza person," the email began, and then Benin addressed several of the top complaints they'd received.

For example:

Long Processing Times

This is an overtold story. We are growing quick, more folks are loving Graza, and we need to step up to the plate to make sure our fulfillment and processing grows accordingly. We have the stock, and we promise to get orders out rapidly all of 2023.

I hope that you stick it out with us on this crazy ride, because damn is Graza tasty, loveable, and fun to use, and I assure you that we will back all of that up with excellence all around our business moving forward. As a small gesture (and keep in mind that this email is going out to 10's of thousands of people and we are a 11 month old 5 person business LOL), I've created a code wewillgetbetter for $4.43 off any future order (this is truly what we can afford!).[19]

The email, errors and all, was sent to 35,544 customers with a 78 percent open rate (that's bonkers), and within minutes the responses started flooding in—to the tune of nearly one thousand of them.

I won't be using the discount, but I will be reordering.

These messages go a long way.

In a world where some leaders are getting busted for using AI to write their crisis emails and apologies, Graza did the opposite. The CEO sent an honest, transparent message, telling the story of the struggle from one human to another, and the marketplace responded—including the journalist who was on the receiving end of one of the disappointing orders of leaked oil and ungiftable gifts.

At first the journalist was disheartened, and then he received the email. "It didn't just win me back," Ben Cohen of the *Wall Street Journal* reported. "It made me more likely to buy more Graza." The next time he was in the store and saw one of the squeezable Graza bottles, he came home with some affordable olive oil, fit for royalty.[20]

When it comes to building trust and influencing action, sometimes the best story is the one told right in the middle of the chaos. Full transparency, all the authenticity.

TELL STORIES OF THE HARDEST PART
TO HELP EMERGING LEADERS

Let's switch gears for a moment—from olive oil to medicine. In a field where logic and deep knowledge are not only encouraged but required, storytelling is not a broadly utilized strategy for teaching in the medical field. Though it is a profession *filled* with stories, they are considered inefficient, anti-scientific—especially when compared to rigorous clinical trials—and, in many cases, are openly discouraged. However, even in the most unwelcome environment, medicine, researchers have recognized the value of storytelling, particularly in the teaching and passing on of values and attitudes from experienced clinicians to aspiring ones.

A report titled "Storytelling as a Method for Teaching Values and Attitudes," published in the journal *Academic Medicine*, explored this phenomenon and lamented the limitations inherent in the prevailing approach to educating future caregivers:

> The teaching of knowledge and skills is the central focus of the present system. No one doubts these things are important; but in the race to teach facts and skills, the teaching of values and attitudes is largely ignored. The result: students learn the skills and knowledge needed to solve problems but are ill-equipped to deal with the ethical and moral dilemmas that problem solving generates.[21]

This shortfall is not just a problem for the medical field but in businesses everywhere. So much training is focused on the "what to dos" and "how to do its" that very little is spent on the gray matter.

The ethics, values, and attitudes. The emotional toll and mental fatigue. The culture. The "what it really means to be a part of this team, to do this work . . . the good, the bad, the ugly." When it comes to complex, nuanced work, regardless of field or industry, knowledge and skill are only part of it. As the research reported in medical training, so it is true in all professions . . . when it comes to raising leaders who understand and can thrive in the wholeness of their career and calling, stories play a critical role.

Of all the academic papers and research studies I devoured in the writing of this book, this article was my favorite. As one would expect from medical professionals, the concepts presented were thorough, straightforward, and definitive. But perhaps the *most* exciting thing about it was how "non-medical" it was. A fact even the article acknowledged:

> As surely as physicians must continue to learn new knowledge and skills, so also must they continue their moral development, in order to cope with the endless dilemmas the practice of medicine presents. . . . Although as a teaching method storytelling runs counter to traditional medical education, if it is used properly, educators will find their teaching more rewarding, their students more interesting, and their own education more complete.[22]

In other words: There is immense value, even in a precise, highly scientific environment in the story being told. And not just any story, according to the study, but one type of story stood out. The story of the hardest part of the job.

After years of experience, it is well-documented that young physicians face two main crises early in their careers:

1. The crisis of professionalization (encountering the many painful "firsts" of the profession), and

2. The crisis of the doctor-patient relationship.

Both shape young clinicians in profound and not always positive ways, and both serve as "fertile ground for experienced physicians to share the stories, preferably of their own struggles," and in doing so, offer important perspective during a formative time. Clarifying the two common challenges that every incoming person to the profession faces gave direction to the experienced physicians and made it easier to identify which stories to find and tell first.[23]

Just as Uncle Ben told Spider-Man, with great power comes great responsibility and with great responsibility comes a lot of hard stuff that's unpleasant to endure (though that last part was inferred rather than stated). Just as the experienced physicians learned in the above study, in telling the stories of the challenges your emerging leaders are likely to encounter, you equip them. Not just with knowledge, but with a deeper understanding of what to expect emotionally, morally and beyond. Additionally, when they find themselves in those moments where skills aren't enough, emerging leaders who have been told the stories of the "hardest parts of the job" will feel less alone and more willing to ask for guidance. They'll understand the discomfort not as an anomaly or personal failure, but rather as a part of the job that others can help to overcome.

STRATEGY #2:
ANTICIPATE THE CRISES
THEY MIGHT FACE

If you are a leader responsible for raising other leaders (and if that's *not* currently your responsibility, you should *make* it your responsibility), sit down and ask yourself this question:

What will be the two hardest things about their job?

Think back on your experience. What would you say were the two things that kept you up at night that you never saw coming when you showed up for your first day on the job? Perhaps one is dealing with challenging customers. Perhaps you only deal with the best of the best—the highly educated and extremely wealthy, and you *assumed* this would make customer interaction easier when the opposite was true. The customers required *more* time, effort, and emotional investment as a result of their education and wealth and you spend most of your time proving your worth and easing irrational concerns. Tell the stories of those customers—choose a few of them—and leave no detail untold, no emotion unshared.

Or perhaps the hardest part of your job is the oppressive quotas. It's a sales role, and you expected that . . . but what you didn't expect was the company's tendency to constantly redraw territory borders and "reward" high performers with higher levels to perform to. It can be motivating . . . it can also be exhausting. Tell the story of the first time your quota was raised and how, after the initial shock, you rose to the challenge (implying that they can too!).

Or maybe the hardest thing about the job is that there is so much travel that they won't even be able to keep a plant alive, much less a pet, friendship, or romantic relationship. Yes, they can watch George Clooney in *Up in the Air* . . . but hearing your #roadwarrior story will serve them much better. Especially if those stories include a little humor and tips on how to manage it all.

Will the hardest part of their job be office politics? Is there one person who makes everything feel impossible? The dispatch manager Roz in *Monsters, Inc.* comes to mind. Maybe it's the gatekeeper of the CEO's office or the head of accounting. Maybe the regional director has a chip on their shoulder or the chief legal counsel takes months to turn even the simplest contract around. Or, as it can for physicians, does a mistake mean someone lives or dies?

Choose the two hardest things they'll have to face, and then, with all the transparency you have in you . . .

Tell them *your* answer to that prompt, *your* version of that story.

What did it look like the day *you* first came face-to-face with the hardest thing about your job?

What happened to *you* the day that hard thing almost took you out?

Know what these stories are. Then be prepared to tell them—transparently, authentically, truthfully—and watch the impact it makes and the wave of positive influence it creates.

There's no doubt that influence is an important piece of leadership.

But now that we mention it, inspiration is pretty essential too.

Inspire the people; tell the story.

That's what we'll tackle next.

EIGHT

Operation Inspiration

*"After nourishment, shelter and companionship,
stories are the thing we need most in the world."*
—PHILIP PULLMAN

To some, becoming an "inspirational leader" may seem like too soft an objective. To others, it might feel like too lofty a goal. In this chapter we'll explore not only *how* you can use Truth 2: *The story needs to be told* to become an inspirational leader, but exactly *why* you should invest energy into this endeavor.

By the time you finish this chapter, you'll learn about just a few of the many ways Truth 2—*tell the story*—can make an inspirational impact, including:

- Telling stories to inspire engagement

- Telling stories to inspire creativity

- Telling stories to inspire problem-solving

- Telling stories to inspire belief

TELL THE STORY TO
INSPIRE ENGAGEMENT

Something has changed at work. You no doubt have felt it, especially if you lead a team. In the past, ambitious new hires would ask for promotions nearly as soon as their cubicle was assigned. Now managers have to actively seek out and convince employees it's time to move up (and many decline). In one survey of over one thousand HR employees, "Forty-five percent said their organization has struggled more than usual to motivate employees to work beyond the required scope of their job in the past six months."[1] The reason for this decline in motivation and productivity? Economists are pointing to worker disengagement as a major factor.

Major *and* majorly expensive; when an employee leaves, that's when the organization really starts to pay. Gallup reported that voluntary turnover costs US companies $1 trillion per year (and that was being conservative).[2] To fill the gaps in their teams, Statista reported companies spent anywhere from forty-six to seventy-two hours training a single new employee in 2022,[3] while Oracle claims that even after all that training, "on average, it takes a new hire one to two years to reach the productivity of an existing employee."[4] Not to mention the hit to morale and its impact on future performance.

Perhaps you've heard the logic that hate isn't the opposite of love, indifference is . . . and it seems across industries, organizations are dealing with workforces that don't "hate" their jobs—they just don't really care anymore.

Herein lies one of the biggest opportunities of the modern leader: figure out how to engage, or re-engage, or keep engaged your team . . . and the rest all gets easier. Those organizations with engaged employees enjoy benefits including, but not limited to: improved morale, retained institutional knowledge, improved productivity, improved corporate culture and customer experience, and better employee engagement/satisfaction.[5] All of these factors, in turn, help to optimize revenue, create a better brand reputation and a more positive company culture, and build a highly skilled workforce.[6]

In short, today's leaders must not only produce but also engage.

So how does a leader inspire engagement?

You'll be shocked by the answer, I'm sure . . .

Tell the stories.

THE SECRET OF ENGAGEMENT:
STORY FLUENCY

In 2018, inspired by a study designed to test resilience in youth based on how many stories they knew of their family's history, my team created a similar study that explored the correlation between an employee's "story fluency" (how many stories they knew of their leaders and company history) and various aspects that impact thriving organizations and teams, including employee engagement.

We administered a national survey to one thousand full-time US employees ranging from eighteen to sixty-five years old. Of those surveyed who measured as Story Fluent, meaning they knew many stories about their leaders and company, 81.2 percent of them also reported being active or engaged in their company's purpose, cause, culture, and team.

Yes. Those employees who had been told the stories were also the employees most engaged.

Said another way: the more stories they knew, the more engaged the employees were.

It makes sense. Now more than ever, people want to feel *connected to* and *inspired by* and find *meaning in* the work they do. They want to feel aligned with the values of the company and what it stands for. Unfortunately, "all too often leaders assume that if they continually recite their organization's values, the words will take on an incantatory power, and employees will fall under their spell, almost like zombies."[7]

You do not want zombies working for you. You want engaged, *inspired* (and alive) people. In order to achieve that, leaders must be *telling the stories* that are *behind* the values. Or the stories of those values in action.

In my firm's 2018 research study, the survey questions included:

Do you know the story of how the company you work for started/came to be?

Do you know if the company you work for has ever faced challenges or setbacks in its history?

Our results revealed that participants who answered yes to those two questions alone were 40 percent more likely to affirm "the work we do at the company makes a difference in the world."

Two stories! Just knowing those two stories meant experiencing more meaning in the work they do.

If you're a leader who's been trying to figure out how to overcome the Zombie-Employment-Apocalypse and the apathy that is threatening to destroy the modern workplace, here are a few strategies to help now that you know *a story needs to be told.*

STRATEGY #3:
LOOK BACK TO GET AHEAD

We talked about this in the previous chapter in reference to exploring your own life stories—that it's likely you spend most of your time thinking about the future, preparing for it, executing on it, and setting the next future goal. However, now that you know Story Fluency will help increase engagement, foster alignment, and create more meaningful work environments, your first job is figuring out what your company stories even *are*. Leaders must do a full excavation on the company's past, including the stories of the early days and the reasons why and how the company came to be. And I'm not the only one who will tell you that's the case.

"Corporate history can be a strategic and motivational resource," says Ranjay Gulati, a professor of Business Administration at Harvard Business School who has spent decades researching companies around the world. Although many experts regard the past as "a hindrance to innovation," Gulati believes that's not entirely true but rather, "Treated as a reference point for thought and action, it can actually drive progress in a way that provides continuity and offers stakeholders a sense of identity, pride, and responsibility as custodians of a legacy."

Take LEGO, for example.

"For two years in the 2000s, Jørgen Vig Knudstorp, then the CEO of the LEGO Group, delved deep into the then-70-year-old company's archives, studied the life of its founder, Ole Kirk Christiansen, and met with long-serving employees."[8] Two *whole* years. Imagine. A CEO turning down important meetings because he had to go find some stories?! It seems preposterous and yet, look at LEGO now.

In June of 2022, *CEO* magazine reported that "LEGO is the world's biggest toy company, with a market value exceeding US$9 billion . . . In 2021, a group of international business researchers found that investing in LEGO was more lucrative than gold, stocks, art or wine."[9] Sharing the values and convictions of LEGO—like facilitating learning and intellectual growth through "good play"—likely became more compelling and effective when Knudstorp could tell the *stories* he uncovered in his research. Knowing these stories created a worldwide organization so engaged that it can turn out "seven toy brick sets passing through the world's checkouts every single second."[10] That's 600,000 LEGO sets a *day*. (And I'm pretty sure at least fifty of them are poured out on my kids' bedroom floors at any given time.)

TELL THE STORY
TO INSPIRE CREATIVITY

Creativity is key to business success; that's no surprise to you. But have you ever considered why this is the case? Creativity allows for nonlinear thinking, daydreaming that inspires new products and services, new ways of approaching a market, engaging with customers, and opening doors to new parts of the world. And sadly, as adults, we often don't get enough creative opportunities. As kids we play and explore. We paint or color (or build with LEGO bricks) or play dress-up, but then as grown-ups . . . we just don't. We're supposed to "get it right"; there is a pressure to "perform," so there's not a whole lot of room for creativity. Which means inspiring creativity, especially among people who have had it trained out of them, is tough.

Telling stories helps.

Lauren Blanco of Markham & Fitz stumbled upon the power of storytelling and creativity and got some delicious results. I know this because when I originally reached out to her, I was in search of a story behind the story. And that's what I got . . . but not in the way I expected.

I was recently in an upscale grocery store in my neighborhood on the Upper East Side of Manhattan. I was there to buy fish for dinner—but of course, they route you through all sorts of shelves and past all the extra things they want you to buy even though you don't need them before you get to the checkout counter, and one of the items I passed was a chocolate bar. Now, at the time, I was on a "reset," if you will—and chocolate was definitely *not* on the list of things I could eat (hence the fish). However, the corner of my eye spotted something that my subconscious recognized as a story, and suddenly I was holding a chocolate bar in my hands.

Yes. You read that right. My eye spotted a story . . . and it was also a chocolate bar.

A chocolate bar *wrapped* in a story. The story was printed on the packaging and stopped me in my don't-look-at-anything-because-you're-doing-a-reset-and-can-only-eat-fish-and-broccoli tracks:

> My mom, it turns out, has the rare gift of larger-than-life enthusiasm. A collegiate gymnast turned fitness professional, she opened an aerobics studio in the 1980s, ripe with spandex, high kicks and bouncing energy . . .

Suddenly I was no longer strolling down a grocery aisle, I was drawn in. I wanted to know more about this person's energetic mother. Even as I read it in passing I imagined what the studio looked like, conjuring images of the aerobics classes I took at LA Fitness in the early 2000s.

There was a "dot dot dot" signaling that you needed to turn the chocolate bar over to read the rest. So I did. But much to my dismay, only *part* of the story was visible on the backside of the packaging—and it said something about "when I was born" and "Richard Simmons Energy to childhood . . ." Reading the *rest* of the story required *unwrapping* the chocolate, something I figured would be frowned upon unless you planned to actually *purchase* it. As I contemplated the purchase of the single chocolate story, I noticed it wasn't just *one* chocolate bar story; there was a whole *series* of flavors, each wrapped in a different story.

That was it for me.

The chocolate I could resist. The stories, I could not.

Though once I got the bars home, it turns out, I couldn't resist the chocolate either. The flavors were like nothing I'd ever seen or tried before.

Smoke & Brulee. Lemon Poppyseed.

Award-winning flavors, in fact.

This I discovered when, unable to be satisfied by the chocolate and the stories on the wrapper alone, I got in touch with Lauren Blanco, cofounder and CEO of Markham & Fitz Chocolate Makers. As I mentioned, initially I reached out to see if the stories on the wrappers resulted in higher sales (or being able to demand a higher price point because the grocery store in my neighborhood was selling them for a breathtaking twenty dollars a bar—which is why I only bought two). She didn't really have the stats on that, but instead shared something much more valuable.

It was stories that led to the flavors in the first place.

After 2020, Lauren, like many of us, was struggling on a more existential level. Business was plugging along and she was doing her "job" making chocolate and leading a team, but something seemed to be missing.

"I found myself asking *why*. Why am I even doing this?"

Lauren started writing. Writing about the people in her life who made her fall in love with food. Her mother. Her grandfather. Trips to New Orleans. A special cake. And, of course, chocolate. She found as she started writing these stories, possible flavors started to emerge.

"It was like a creative explosion!" she said, which was much welcomed after a challenging few years. Experiencing the power of revisiting her own life stories to unlocking dormant creativity, she brought the exercise to her team. They sat around and each shared some of their favorite food memories—bonding and connecting and the collision of different stories created entirely new flavors to explore.

"In the food industry, it is all about achieving satisfaction for the person on the receiving end of what you've made," Lauren explained. "And satisfaction is entirely related to experience . . ."

"And experience is all about story," I finished.

In the end, when trying to design a wrapper for the chocolate bars whose flavors were inspired by Lauren's stories, traditional artwork just didn't seem to do it justice. "And then one day we thought, *Well . . . what if we just print the story?*"

That is how the Origin Stories line of chocolate came to be. And it worked, because when I went back to my grocery store to spend another fortune on chocolate . . . the bars were gone.

The moral of the story? You never know what creativity a little story exchange will inspire. As a leader, build time in to allow these stories to be told.

STORIES TO INSPIRE PROBLEM-SOLVING

"Are there any questions?" the facilitator asked the room. You could hear the crowd shift in their seats. Oh, they had questions. The *real* question was, *Where should we begin?*

It was the fall of 2023 and I was in the audience of a women's leadership conference where I would be speaking later that afternoon. In the room were approximately two hundred women from every area of the global health company: Research & Development, Quality Control, and more.

It was a day of leadership and growth with a strong undertone of personal empowerment. The organization was clearly aware that within the ranks of their colleagues there was a trove of untapped potential. The event felt like an unstated acknowledgment of the hibernating greatness within each of the women in the room, and the desire among everyone to unlock and release that potential was palpable.

The day kicked off with a presentation from a special guest speaker—a C-Suite executive—and the audience hung on every word of his brief presentation. There was barely a delay after his talk before the first hand was in the air and a woman in the middle of the room was handed a microphone to ask her question.

"How do you grow leaders to prepare for a crisis?"

Every head in the room swiveled, including my own, from the woman asking the question to the man on the stage. It was the question everyone wanted to ask because if *anyone* had the answer . . . it was him.

In his role, the executive leads a global team to ensure consistent adherence to the company's quality, regulatory, and engineering values. Strict compliance to global requirements, highest-quality products for customers, and a safe environment for the organization's colleagues who work in every corner of the planet all fall under his guidance.

When he started in the role, the executive knew he was walking into a big job but was confident he was ready for it. Not only did he have just shy of thirty years' experience with the organization, the job itself was well-established and, as a whole, it was a notoriously by-the-books company.

Certainly, it wouldn't be *easy*—there was a lot to it even on a good day—but the seasoned executive was essentially taking the wheel of a well-oiled machine ready for smooth sailing ahead.

He started in November 2019.

On December 12, 2019, a group of patients in Wuhan, China, reported falling ill with symptoms similar to pneumonia but that did not respond to standard treatments. One month on the job and suddenly the waters of his new, smooth-sailing job got choppy. Very, *very* choppy.

Suddenly, the executive had a very big problem with almost zero precedence for how to solve it.

"How do you grow leaders to be prepared for crisis?" He repeated the question. He paused as, one can only assume, the past three-plus years flashed before his eyes, before answering, "You can never be 'prepared' for *that*." The mood in the room shifted slightly, as if you could hear the pens of two hundred overachieving, ultra-planning, hyper-focused women stop mid-sentence. You can never *prepare*?!

He knew his audience well enough to quickly continue.

"We had never conceptualized a crisis of that magnitude. There were no models, no precedence for what happened in 2020." I pictured their previous playbooks. The processes and procedures that had been developed over the decades of the company's experience. I imagined the executive pulling binders out of file cabinets, furiously flipping through pages trying to find the chapter with guidance for being a worldwide medical device organization in the middle of a "Complete Global Shutdown." Pretty sure there weren't routes to run or plays to anticipate.

"The best way to prepare is to build belief in yourself," he said simply.

It was simple yet profound. And he was right. The best way to prepare to succeed in a time of crisis is to *believe* you can succeed in a time of crisis.

Fostering an environment that encourages team members to solve problems—especially compared to just noticing them—will be the make-or-break moment for thriving in an era when anything could happen. A culture focused on *solutions* can cultivate individual commitment to a project's outcomes, empower employees to avoid analysis paralysis, and ultimately shorten the lifespan of the problems a company faces.[11] You'll be relieved to know that our research revealed, much like Story Fluent employees were more engaged, nearly 83 percent of those employees who had been told and knew many of their company's and leaders' stories also reported that at their company, people worked together to solve problems.

If you want a team that can solve any problem, they must first believe they can solve any problem. In order to help them believe they can solve any problem, go back to the stories of the problems that have been solved.

STRATEGY #4:
TELL THE STORIES OF
PROBLEMS SOLVED

It's perhaps not pleasant to go back and revisit the biggest challenges or obstacles or potentially devastating moments in your company's history, but if you ended up solving the problem and came through on the other side, you've got a story to tell.

Search back through your memory, your calendar, ask more senior employees: What were some of the biggest problems faced and how did they end up getting solved? Were they resolved by the team or by a certain individual?

Go ahead, dive all the way into how impossible the situation was—in fact, the more impossible the better—because that story can be told to remind the team that no problem will go unsolved.

And while belief in the ability to solve problems is important, so is building belief, period.

STRATEGY #5:
TELL THE STORIES OF HOW
GREAT THEY ARE TO INSPIRE
SELF-CONFIDENCE

On an episode of his popular podcast series about coaches, Michael Lewis told the story of his high school baseball coach. Not a big podcast listener myself, my husband, a person who attributes many life lessons to the influence of his tough-love high school water polo coach, sent me the episode as I was working on this chapter.

"You should listen to this," he said.

He's usually right.

So one afternoon, struggling to overcome a mean case of writer's block, I decided to take a "working break." I put in my headphones, turned on the episode, and listened as I mowed the lawn. And I was captivated.

Lewis, famed author of nonfiction blockbusters such as *Moneyball*, *The Blind Side*, and *The Big Short*, revealed that as a fourteen-year-old boy, he was a complete mess.

"To say that I'm troubled isn't quite right. Inert is more like it," he explained, thinking back. He had zero interest in anything—his teachers couldn't motivate him, and even his mother broke down in frustration and basically bemoaned that he was ruining her life.

"My mom's great," he said. "It's not her fault. I just didn't much care about anything except performing the occasional acts of vandalism." And then he was asked to join the summer baseball team by Coach Bill Fitzgerald—the kind of coach legends are made of. The kind that could make grown men and high school boys cry.

That particular summer, their team was actually pretty good. But the night of the story, Lewis's team was playing the only other team in the league that could beat them. And, to make matters worse, the coach pulled the older, better pitcher in the final inning and put Lewis in. The barely budding Lewis was already no match for the other team—guys with facial hair and muscles—but to top it off they put him in with runners on first and third base and his team only trailing by one run. Things suddenly started to look very bad for the otherwise apathetic teenager.

As Lewis walked toward the mound, Coach Fitz looked him in the eye and said: "There is no one I'd rather have in this situation." Looking back, Lewis is certain it was a lie, "but such is the force of the man" that he believed "every word." Coach said a few more words, what to do about the guy on third, handed Lewis the ball, and walked away from the mound. Whatever the coach said had worked. Lewis pitched a strong final inning and his team won the game. "But that's not the full magic of this moment. The magic is what Billy Fitzgerald uses it to do."

It is this next part, I realized as I was pushing my electric mower straight up the hill in our front yard, that is the reason my husband suggested I give this episode a listen. He was right.

> After the game, [Coach Fitz] gives a little speech to the team about the nature of courage and how, if you wanna know what it looks like, you just need to watch me pitch.
>
> I'm hearing myself being described in an entirely original way and wanting to believe it . . . what that coach did in that moment was to hand me the start of a new identity by giving me a new narrative.
>
> I was no longer this pointless human being, this nightmare of inertia. I was brave, a hero almost. And I ran with it. Four years later when the letter arrives saying that I'd gotten into Princeton, I run to the school to find Coach Fitzgerald to let him know. Not to say look what I did, to say look what you made it possible for me to do.[12]

Certainly, the people you are tasked with leading in an office setting are probably not fourteen-year-olds trying to survive those awkward days (weeks, years) before becoming adults. However, that does not mean that they are less uncertain, or at least influenced by the way people they respect see them.

For this reason, like the coach in the story, some of the most important stories you can tell are their own stories back to them.

Pay attention to the moments when your team members exhibited excellence.

Keep a file of the big and small ways you witnessed their greatness.

Tell the story of the first time you met them and what you thought—did you think they wouldn't stick and you were wrong? Did you think they'd be great and they've proved you right? Did you already think they were great and then there was this one time when they showed you how badly you underestimated that greatness?

Tell those stories.

Tell them in a public forum for the rest of the team to hear.

Tell them quietly at a time when you notice they're questioning themselves.

Tell them through your own eyes and with an authentic sense of wisdom and wonder.

Never underestimate the positive impact you can make on a person, how they see themselves, and ultimately, who they become simply by telling them one of their own stories.

Lewis, now one of the most successful American authors with several books-turned-movies, can attest to this: "Of one thing I am totally certain; if I'd never met Coach Fitz, I'd have never become a writer. It would have felt too risky, too hard."

And it's a good thing Lewis became a writer because years later, when Coach Fitz was at risk of being fired because parents were offended by his "tough love" approach, Lewis wrote an article for the *New York Times Magazine* and told the story of the leader who shaped the man Lewis had become. The article generated overwhelming outrage—"Not towards the coach . . . towards the people hoping to get the coach fired. They got run outta town more or less. The headmaster left the school, too, and the school created a committee to find a new headmaster and put Coach Billy Fitzgerald in charge of it."

Yes, lack of engagement and losing employees is expensive in time, money, and all the other ways we use to measure value in business. Productivity, creativity, and effective problem-solving are all essential. However, more than the financial and efficiency benefits of keeping your team together, the reward for making a difference in the way a person sees it is priceless.

TELL STORIES—INSPIRE THE MASSES

There is a story to be told.

This is the battle cry of the Story Forward Leader.

"There is something to be done . . . and story will be the thing to do it!" It is part of the reason Story Forward Leaders are inspirational leaders, why their legacies live on long after they're gone.

I first heard the SBCA story when Paul Mauger sent me an email after reading my first book. The subject line read: *$1.2M Success Story to Share.* The first line said simply: *I am sold on the art of story-telling! I would like to share one example of where this has proved successful for me.*

Naturally, I wanted to read more and was completely entranced by the incredible story he spun about sharing a story . . . and I even suggested one edit: that maybe his subject line for the email should not have been about "$1.2M" but rather "Future Lives Saved." However, it was the last few lines of his email that were the most powerful.

"My dad was a master at telling stories," Paul wrote. "He had the ability to 'build the bridge' with people like few others could. . . .

His funeral was one of the largest attended in his community. I even had a person introduce himself to me and explain that he had worked for my dad. He proceeded to share that my dad fired him. In my shock I asked why he came to his funeral? He replied, 'I deserved it, he was the best supervisor I ever worked for.'"

Clearly, Paul's father was a Story Forward Leader long before it was a term in a business book. And I, personally, am a little sad I missed the opportunity to meet him—a man whose funeral was attended both by people he loved and people he fired.

Leave your legacy.

Tell the stories.

YOU'RE ALWAYS IN THE MIDDLE OF THE STORY

How Leaders Activate
Optimism and Resilience to
Overcome Any Challenge

NINE

Smack Dab
in the Middle

"What are we except a bunch of stories . . . ?"
—ANN PATCHETT

To be a sports fan is to open your heart to great excitement and euphoria, devastating pain and suffering—all within the span of a few hours. Whether it's on a field or a court, whether the ball is kicked or pitched or thrown or hit, at their best, games pull us into their plots.

A recent study by a work outplacement firm determined that March Madness, the NCAA college basketball tournament, resulted in a collective $17.3 billion in lost productivity alone.[1] Individual games and months-long seasons chew us up with anticipation and spit us out with unpredictable wins and heartbreaking losses. As a fan, watching the story unfold is intense.

So imagine, for a moment, the intensity of what it takes to be *inside* the story, playing instead of just watching a game. I found

myself contemplating this very fact after the NFC North championship game in December 2022, when the Minnesota Vikings managed to pull off the biggest comeback in NFL history.

I am no stranger to the emotional whiplash that comes with being
a Vikings fan. It's in my blood. My grandmother famously remembered the names of the Vikings players long after she struggled with
the names of her grandchildren. She loved to hate them (the Vikings,
not her grandchildren) and hated to love them to the very end.

The sound of the Vikings game on my father's radio as he worked
in the garage and his subsequent grumbling at missed plays and
squandered leads was the soundtrack of my childhood.

So, when the Vikings showed up on their home field on that
fateful day late in 2022 to play the game that would seal their play-
off fate, and not only didn't score *anything* in the first half, but
allowed their opponents, the Indianapolis Colts, to post thirty-three
points . . . the story seemed all but over. *No one can come back from
that* echoed in the minds of Colts fans, Vikings fans, and one can
only assume the players too. Because no team in the history of football ever had come back from a 33–0 deficit at halftime.

I will spare you the lowlights of the first half. Plays were missed,
plays were made, and when the clock ran down, both teams jogged
off the field to their respective locker rooms. What happened next is
a master class in the impact of Truth 3: *You're always in the middle of
the story.*

You're not at the beginning.

You're not at the end.

You are in the middle.

In an interview with NFL Network Insider Tom Pelissero, Vikings
quarterback Kirk Cousins recounted the moment in the locker room
when things changed, and a victory even seemed possible.

"Patrick Peterson said all we needed was five touchdowns. I thought he was being sarcastic . . ." Cousins recalled.

Vikings head coach Kevin O'Connell seconded the sentiment. "Patrick Peterson, I'll never forget it for as long as I live," O'Connell said. "I walked out to address the team before we went back out there, and I just overheard him walk over toward the offense [and] said, 'We're going to get stops. You just need five touchdowns. That's nothing.'"[2]

Halftime concluded and both teams returned to the field. Two quarters and an overtime later, the Vikings had pulled off the greatest comeback in NFL history.

No doubt, part of what made that turnaround possible is the innate essence required of an elite athlete. It's the physical and mental conditioning to strategize until the very end—finding ways to outsmart and outplay the other team. The hours and hours of tapes they'd watched had trained them to evaluate what worked and what didn't and to adjust quickly.

However, what happened in that moment was not just the result of physical training; it was the result of a leader who understands, has practiced, and has fostered an attitude of optimism and honed the dynamic process of resilience—both of which are necessary for business excellence and both of which are embodied within this final Truth by which the Story Forward Leader lives.

A truth that, sadly, often gets thwarted by a defunct inner-story compass, leaving us lost in our own stories. You see, cornerback Patrick Peterson knew the story wasn't over; they were figuratively (and literally) just in the middle of it.

YOU ARE HERE

Like the blue dot that shows your location on Google Maps or the red dot on a mall directory or a yellow star on a map of a wilderness trail, the third Truth for Story Forward leadership insists a leader always know where they are—not, of course, their physical location, but rather where they are *in the story*.

And I've got good news for you. It's not a secret location: you're in the same place as everyone you know (and, in fact, everyone you don't know). You don't have to keep track of your location, because it never changes. In fact, the only challenging part is fighting the sometimes-overwhelming urge to believe that you are somewhere else, in a different part of the story.

So, where exactly are you?

You're in the middle.

TRUTH 3:
YOU'RE ALWAYS IN THE
MIDDLE OF THE STORY

Take a moment to let that settle in: you are in the middle of the story. At any given moment, in any aspect of your life and work, anywhere on the continuum of your company's life and evolution or the perpetuity of your career, you're in the middle. Whether you're reading this after successfully crossing a huge finish line or at a moment when you're struggling to get started, you're in the middle of a story. Not at the beginning. Not at the end.

And though understanding you're in the middle is a *good thing*, the middles of stories are our least favorite places to be. Because of our deep dislike for the middle, we've conditioned ourselves to simply not accept that that's where we actually are and, instead, we approach any given situation that isn't living up to our expectations or standards as either an End or a Beginning. The result is a permanent state of disorientation that leads to adverse results, or, at the very least, puts us in a position that makes reaching our potential or meeting our goals much more difficult than it needs to be.

Like Patrick Peterson at halftime of that fateful game, you are here and you are in the middle. It's a place where optimism can be maintained and resilience expressed even while navigating both the big tidal waves and the smaller inconveniences of business. Middles of stories are powerful, if not a little chaotic, places to be, yet we often miss the benefits of keeping that middle-mentality because our internal cartographic abilities are flawed in two fundamental ways:

1. We think we're at the *end* of a story (when really . . . it's the middle), or

2. We think we're at the *beginning* of a story (when really . . . it's the middle).

Why are we so directionally challenged when it seems quite simple?

Let's explore further and begin with why we often think we're at the *end* of a story instead of in the middle. To explain this phenomenon, we need look no further than our relationship with uncertainty.

THE PROBLEM WE HAVE
WITH WHAT WE DO NOT KNOW

Did you know there are people who always read the *last* page of a book *first*?!

I recently posted this question on social media: "Do you read the last page of a book first, and if so, why?"

Some of my respondents were shocked and appalled at the thought of it. One person even said reading the last page first was "sacrilegious." And then there were others (perhaps you're one of them) who freely admitted that they often skip to the end before reading the beginning. What I found most interesting, after asking the people who start at the end, were their reasons why. Or more accurately, their *reason*. Although they said it in different ways, it all came down to the fact that they felt discomfort about the unknown. They were anxious and felt that, unless they skipped ahead, they would feel a total lack of control.

Here are a few of their responses:

"I just can't stand not knowing."

"I need to know where we are going. I need to know how the journey ends. I can't concentrate unless I know how it ends or at least have an idea of where it's going."

"I feel out of control by not knowing."

"I'm the type of person who rewatches movies over and over again too. I guess I just need to know what's happening or else I get too anxious."

"Sometimes I will start a book and I need to know if my favorite character lives or dies, so I skip to the end. I need to prepare myself."

Perhaps the most succinct answer came from my friend Amy Morin, a psychotherapist and multi-bestselling author of the 13 Things Mentally Strong People Don't Do series.

Amy wrote:

> I don't like uncertainty. So I like to read the end of the
> book the same way I Google how a TV season ends or
> know who the murderer is in the mystery before I check
> it out. Then I can just sit back and relax and enjoy the
> book without being distracted by thoughts like, "Ooh, I
> wonder if they get back together." Weird, right? But I
> think, for me, it's like the one time in life where I *can*
> know the future before it happens, and I like it.

The essence of the issue is right there in her first sentence: "I don't
like uncertainty." And though you may not be the kind of person
who reads the end of a book first, you, too, likely have a complicated
relationship with uncertainty. All humans do. In fact, studies have
shown that we find uncertainty more stressful than actual negative
outcomes.

For example, researchers conducted a study in which subjects
faced a potential electric shock, with each round offering a varying
probability of the shock being administered. You might assume that
the most stressful rounds would be those in which subjects faced
100 percent certainty of being shocked, but that assumption would
be wrong. In the study, subjects experienced the highest levels of
stress when there was a 50 percent chance that they might receive a
shock.[3]

Another study found that anxious individuals had a tendency to
select gambling tasks with results that were immediately available,
even when they provided smaller relative payouts and worse odds,
because they minimized the period during which they'd be *uncertain*
of their wins and losses.[4]

Much like those who flip to the back of the book first, our innate desire to reduce or avoid uncertainty drives us to favor *endings*. So much so that if a current situation is too uncomfortable as a result of the unknown, we will seek to prematurely deem the "middle of a story" the "end of the story," just to escape the oppressive anxiety. Instead of leaning into the uncertain middle, knowing that there is a chance the shock might *not* come or the game might *not* be lost, we shake our heads and hands to say, "This is it. The end," which I'm sure you'll agree is not the best look for a leader.

Now let's examine the second fundamental flaw—the reason we think we're at the *beginning* of a story instead of . . . you guessed it . . . the middle.

FORGETTING HOW FAR YOU'VE COME

Many years ago, I was listening to an interview with a woman I admire. She was wildly successful then and is even more so now; she's someone I often looked to when trying to imagine or model my own career.

During this interview, she told the story of the day she woke up, in her forties, and was completely broke. She detailed how she felt like such a failure that she didn't even want to get out of bed. It was such a poignant story because the contrast between the woman who couldn't get out of bed and the woman she had become was so immense and inspiring and . . . if I'm completely honest, a little discouraging, too.

I remember lamenting to my husband that evening about my lack of a good "struggle story"—a low point from which to push off, a comeback to fuel movement upward and forward. As distorted as it might sound, I bemoaned, "Why couldn't *I* have ever been broke?"

My husband stared at me blankly and when I didn't respond, he said, "Um. Kindra. You *were* broke."

And suddenly it all started coming back to me. The tens of thousands of dollars of student loan debt with no clear career path or income to pay it off. Or the thousands of dollars' worth of IKEA furniture I had foolishly put on a credit card. I sold the furniture on Craigslist after moving in with a friend because I couldn't afford rent on my own (and she already had a futon), and though the furniture was long gone, the minimum credit card payments remained. Or the time the girl at the salon (that I shouldn't have been going to) sold me some fancy shampoo (that I should have said no to), and I overdrew my checking account. Or when I was sitting on my bed on the phone with Netflix, crying to them because I forgot to cancel my monthly $7 DVD subscription before the next month's payment was due, and, yes, I overdrew my checking account . . . again.

Actually, the more I thought about it, I also had spent *a lot* of time on the phone crying to the bank, begging them to give me a break on the overdraft fees. *So* much time that I can still remember exactly how much those fees were—$35—and how relieved I would be when they'd show me some mercy and only charge me $17.50 per transaction. And while I realize my "broke" could have been worse and that it was the result of my own bad decisions and not that of generations of systemic racial or social oppression, personally it was a shameful, stressful, and painful time in my life.

"Wait a minute," I said in shock. "I *was* broke."

My husband nodded. He remembered—we had just started dating when the shampoo debacle occurred.

And that's when it occurred to me: I had completely lost track of my own story. I'd forgotten what I'd struggled through and how far I'd come, and this distortion led me to believe that where I was currently "located" in my story was the *beginning*.

I thought I was at the *beginning* of my story when I heard that interview—and not in a positive, hopeful way, but rather in a "I haven't made any progress toward becoming something *more*" way. By omitting those earlier stories of struggle, I had erased any evidence that I *could* overcome adversity. That I *was* getting better. I had neutralized any power those stories had to fuel belief in myself. I'd lost sight of how resilient I had become.

Certainly, a leader's ability to always look forward, to focus on where they need to go and how they're going to get there, is important, but *only* looking forward undermines resilience. When you're always looking ahead, it's easy to forget how far you've come. You miss rearview opportunities to fuel your motivation, and you deprive others of the honor of seeing what the journey to success really looks like; tears and second-guessing and all.

The night I remembered that I had been broke was a turning point for me. I'd been frantically trying to grow and expand and reach new levels of success and feeling like I wasn't making any progress, or at least not fast enough, when in fact my journey from broke to where I stood and where I stand today was actually pretty inspiring—once I took a moment to see the whole story and realize my location within it: the middle.

EMBRACING THE MIDDLE BUILDS
OPTIMISM AND RESILIENCE

With a desire to further investigate how a middle-of-the-story perspective impacts levels of employee optimism and resilience, if at all, my team and I meticulously administered a national online survey. The survey included four hundred respondents, all of whom were full- or part-time employees with one or more direct reports. Participants were separated, at random, into four groups and presented with one of four versions of a scenario involving a fictitious company called LawnSaber—a manufacturer of lawn equipment. The difference between the groups was as follows:

- Group One reads a challenging business scenario. The story stops before the characters in the story reach a resolution. Group One is given the survey.

- Group Two reads a challenging business scenario. The story is told in its entirety and stops after the characters have reached a resolution. Group Two is given the survey.

- Group Three reads a challenging business scenario. The story stops before the characters reach a resolution— however, the participants are told that there is more to the story, which they'll get to read after answering the survey. Group Three is given the survey. Group Three reads the rest of the story in which the characters reach a resolution.

- Group Four reads a challenging business scenario. The story stops before the characters reach a

resolution—however, the participants are shown one
more paragraph of the story, where the leader of the
company tells his discouraged team a story to assure
them this isn't the end and that the company will come
back stronger than ever. Group Four is given the survey.
Group Four reads the rest of the story in which the
characters reach a resolution.

The survey included acceptable scales designed to measure indicators of optimism and resilience and represented how optimistic
respondents felt about the company and how resilient they would
feel in such a situation.

Not surprisingly, when respondents were given the whole story
(Group Two) and were able to read about LawnSaber's eventual happy
ending, their scores on optimism and resilience were dramatically
higher than those who read about LawnSaber's challenge but weren't
told how the story resolved (Group One). Obviously. Who among
us doesn't feel better after a situation has resolved than we do when
we're in the middle of the mess?! But when it comes to real business
challenges, we *don't* have access to the whole story. We *don't* know
how the story will end until it does. Unless you're sitting on a secret
time machine, you've gotta get through the middles to get to the
end, just like the rest of us.

The more interesting finding of this study was the difference
between Group One, Group Three, and Group Four. Though none
of the participants in these groups knew how or even *if* LawnSaber's
challenges would be resolved (things looked pretty bleak), and
though Group Three was explicitly *told* the story wasn't over yet,
implying that there *could* still be a positive ending, there was no

measurable change in optimism or the propensity for resilience in Group Three as compared to Group One.

However, participants in Group Four, who read the additional paragraph that described the leader sharing a story to draw attention to the fact that LawnSaber's story wasn't over yet, that they were in the middle and the story was still being written—those participants showed an increase in optimism and resilience of 41 percent and 36 percent, respectively, over the control group (Group One).

As a leader who knows how important it is to keep your team focused on what's possible even when facing the impossible, and mentally strong enough to endure the challenge and see it through to resolution—these results should be exciting to you! That optimism and resilience can be impacted through the tenets of Story Forward leadership.

Until widespread access to time machines is available, the following chapters offer more strategies to help you and your team thrive through the middle of your stories.

TEN

Optimism . . . Brought to You by Storytelling

"The direction you choose to face determines whether you're standing at the end or the beginning of a road."
—RICHELLE E. GOODRICH

What *is* optimism, anyway?

Is it wearing so-called "rose-colored glasses" and failing to see the real sadness, injustice, or suffering in the world? Is it just another word, then, for *denial?* Is an optimistic person one who just sunnily claims to be a "glass-half-full" type, ever looking for silver linings? Is optimism the precursor to toxic positivity? Some psychologists call it a coping mechanism. Others claim optimism is a personality trait we're born with, like being more introverted than extroverted. Still others say it's a skill that can be acquired.

One helpful perspective is to take a brief look at growth versus fixed mindsets.

Proposed by world-renowned psychologist Dr. Carol Dweck, who currently teaches at Stanford, this theory describes a mindset as "fixed" when it's inflexible, pessimistic, and assumes that it's the end of the story. Conversely, a person with a "growth mindset" knows they are in the middle of the story, knows there are opportunities for improvement ahead, and knows that things can change.[1]

Think of two students in an elementary school classroom. Both struggle with math. The student with the fixed mindset thinks he's at the end of the story: "I stink at math," he says, while his classmate, a person with a growth mindset (and the same almost-failing grade on the day's math quiz), is thinking, *This isn't the end of the story; I can work to get better.*

It's easy to identify kids with fixed versus growth mindsets. Those with fixed mindsets say things like, "I just can't play the violin" or "I suck at spelling" or "I never score in soccer." They assume they will never improve, never become an expert, and never, ever change. They think they are either good at something . . . or not. Conversely, kids with growth mindsets are hopeful, believe that if they practice they can get better, and have an eye on the future. Challenges for those with growth mindsets are opportunities to . . . well . . . grow.

It's sometimes harder to recognize these mindsets in adults, and certainly takes practice to recognize them in ourselves, but one clue can be whether people see themselves at the end of the story or in the middle. If you're in the middle, things can change, improve, and turn around. If the story is done, well . . . that's that. A person with a fixed mindset believes they're unsuccessful, not as intelligent as their peers, or less gifted; consequently, they don't put time, energy, or effort into improving. It's *done.*

Fully accessing the leadership superpower of optimism requires the leader to know where they are in the story. You're never at the end; you're always in the middle. There is always more story to write.

It is with that spirit and for our purposes that my favorite description of optimism is "the practice of opening yourself up to the vulnerability of hope."

MIDDLE ME ONE MORE TIME.

Several years ago, I randomly found my way to the Instagram account of a musical about princesses that was based solely on the music of Britney Spears. Instantly excited (because Britney's discography and Broadway are two of my favorite things), I searched to find showtimes.

Alas. The show was in Washington, D.C. (I live in New York), and the curtain had already closed on its final performance. I had missed my chance. However, all was not lost because, as often happens when down random social media rabbit holes, I found something else.

The Little Mermaid.

Or rather, the young woman who played the Little Mermaid in the D.C. production. Maybe it was because of her real-life red hair or her willingness to share a behind the scenes look at the life of a Broadway actress . . . whatever the reason, I decided to follow her. Which led to the ultimate lesson in middles versus endings.

According to her posts, she first worked on the show in 2017 when it was in development. For six years and playing three different tracks, she came in and out of that show. They would need her for a while, and then they wouldn't. They would hire her back, and then say goodbye. End. Beginning. End. Oh, never mind . . . beginning!

Oh wait, end. It sounds cruel, but it's pretty much the norm if you dream of being on Broadway.

Saying goodbye to the Mermaid in D.C. was just one more of her endings in a series of farewells spanning *years*.

And then, in the spring of 2023, back in her mermaid costume, she posted that she would be returning to the role when the show opened on Broadway in June.

Did I buy tickets immediately? Yes. Did I take my daughter? Absolutely. Did we have an *amazing* time? Oh yeah. Would I see it again?

I would have . . . but the show closed Labor Day weekend with just over a week's notice. Another ending.

And as I watched the Mermaid's farewell posts—saying goodbye to her castmates, cleaning out her dressing room—I couldn't help but wonder: How does she do it? How can anyone live like that? To have enough hope, enough optimism to not just fully give up at every perceived ending, call it an end, call it a day, and walk away?

Truthfully, to be in the business of Broadway without going crazy requires a deep desensitization to and acceptance of the whims and whipping winds of the tortuous, uncertain middle. You can have the best moves, the biggest voice, even get cast in the best role, win the Tony, and still . . . take your final bow a week later.

The good news is, unless you're a Broadway hopeful of course, that's the extreme. However, fully embracing, embodying, and utilizing the third Story Forward Truth requires becoming more comfortable with uncertainty so that you can resist the urge to think in terms of the *end* of a story, and instead focus on the empowering opportunity of a story that's not yet over. That is the power of optimism . . . that is the *practice* of optimism.

Yes. It is difficult to feel optimistic when so much is changing so rapidly and uncertainty abounds, leaving us feeling exposed and foolish. Foolish to believe you could make a difference, foolish for the team to believe the launch or the account or the project really could be a big deal. To be cynical is to close the door to the possibility of disappointment. To be pessimistic is to foreclose the risk of being made a fool by optimism.[2]

BOBBING IN THE WAVES

"The thing people wanted more than anything was answers." This was the answer given to Lydia Polgreen, opinion columnist at the *New York Times* and former editor in chief at the *Huffington Post*, when she asked her wife, Candace Feit, who went back to school during the pandemic to become a social worker, about her work that focuses on helping people with terminal illness.

Questions about how long their loved one has left or whether or not they're in pain don't have a definitive answer, and it would be irresponsible to pretend that they do. Instead, Feit takes a different approach. "I try to help them increase their tolerance for uncertainty," she explained to Polgreen, who wrote, "In the absence of answers, she tried to help them live with not knowing. We all want to know what happens next, to fix upon some certainty as an anchor in the rough seas of our times. But to tolerate uncertainty is to become buoyant, able to bob in the waves, no matter the tide."[3]

It was that last sentence that inspired me to carry the scrap of newspaper around with me for months. Yes. We like ends. Even if we don't like the ending—a deal not going well, a misguided decision causing a setback, a project failed—it's easier to consider it over and move on.

Like it might have been easier for the Vikings to have chalked the game up as a loss at halftime, simply endured the last two quarters, gone home, and focused on the week to come. But the lesson to learn in all of this is, when things aren't going as planned or hoped for:

There is a difference between showing up as if you're in the middle of a story, and showing up believing the end is already written.

Those who can get comfortable with the uncertain middles of stories are more equipped to keep their heads above water. Knowing you're in the middle of a story = buoyancy. And I'm not the only one who says so.

MAKING SENSE OF THE UNEXPECTED

You know the old adage "There is nothing permanent, except change"?

Research has shown that "storytelling is particularly well-suited for managing the unexpected—not just as an individual, but especially as a group collectively makes sense of something that no one saw coming,"[4] because the process of creating stories is fundamentally constructive in nature. Ultimately, storytelling is a sensemaking activity—not only in retrospect but, more important, as active participants *in* a story as it unfolds, which helps us "discover the actions we must take in order to survive."[5]

By acknowledging that you and your team are in the *middle* of a story and *not* at the end, you unlock the essence of optimism that comes from knowing a story is still being written. The inherent hopefulness that the actions you take, the decisions you make in *this* moment will determine what story is told in the future.

Here are a few exercises to increase your optimism by recentering your location on the story map to the middle.

STRATEGY #1:
TAP INTO MAIN CHARACTER ENERGY

As you might guess, I am a sucker for a story that draws the attention to the story—meta-narratives, if you will. Take, for example, the movie *Enchanted*, in which Amy Adams plays a princess from a storybook who somehow lands in real-world New York City.

Throughout the movie, Adams's character prances through Manhattan, not as if she is one of the millions of people caught up in the rat race, but rather as the main character in an unfolding story, that storybook from which she's come.

Now, I am not suggesting you dance down the Central Park Mall in a princess gown. (Though you *could*, because, as you might know, *anything* goes in New York.) But there *is* a case to be made for embracing the fact that yes, you *are* the main character of your story, and, yes, as you operate in the world moment to moment, your story is being written and, no, unlike those who read the last page of the book first, you cannot know how your story will turn out.

There is a catchphrase for this approach: Main Character Syndrome. Main Character Syndrome generally refers to a person identifying as the protagonist in their own life story.[6] Though I prefer "Main Character *Energy,*" since it's not an actual medical condition.

The phrase first gained notoriety on TikTok as a "specific existential perspective, like realism or pessimism or optimism. It's how you view your life."[7]

Sometimes it's associated with self-centered, egocentric, and narcissistic behaviors. The dark side of Main Character Energy (and maybe this is why some people call it a "syndrome") is entitlement and the belief that you are the center of the universe and everyone else is less important than you.

However, when approached correctly, seeing yourself as the central character of an unfolding story can be a very positive thing. Michael Karson, a professor in the University of Denver's Graduate School of Professional Psychology, stated, "It is healthy to see oneself as the main character of one's own life."[8] Kate Rosenblatt, a therapist and senior clinical manager at Talkspace, echoed the sentiment. "When you view yourself as having agency over your life and that your life and choices are often really up to you," she said, "this can feel powerful and can ultimately contribute to enhanced self-worth, self-esteem, and self-confidence."[9]

How do you tap into your Main Character Energy?

It's by making one simple statement:

"Well . . . let's see how this plays out."

LET'S SEE HOW THIS PLAYS OUT

Once I had decided that the best way to get the word out about the power of storytelling was to speak at events and conferences— reaching the largest number of people in the shortest amount of time—I engaged in the truly soul-sucking work of cold-calling. (Been there? Then you know *exactly* what I mean!)

I set a goal to reach out to a certain number of events, organizations, and conferences each week in the hope that, amid certain rejection (including but not limited to "It's not a good fit" and the even more likely crickets), by sheer number of outreaches I'd get at least a few yeses.

For a time, a few turned out to be the total number. As in, like, six events, maybe seven.

More interesting, though, there was one rejection that, rather than politely decline or simply ignore me, instead sent me a very specific email explaining exactly why they wouldn't consider hiring me for a speaking gig.

Here is an excerpt:

> *To manage your expectations, we rarely hire speakers we haven't approached first. In the past two years, just one out of 30 keynote speakers is someone who pitched us first.*
>
> *Our goal is to provide useful Programming, with high event attendance (130+) as an indicator of success. With that as a benchmark, ideal speakers are people who bring at least two out of the three qualities defined by our association:*
>
> - *Hot Topic*
>
> - *Hot Speaker [a big name]*
>
> - *Hot Brand [a household brand]*
>
> *Storytelling is a hot topic. To get 2 out of 3, your proposal would need to include meat-y, concrete examples from several big-name brands. That's still a stretch, though, since we see stronger attendance when the brand itself presents or co-presents.*

Perhaps the detail of the rejection was designed to be helpful, but I'll be honest, it mostly just felt like someone (who mentioned they were also a "speaker") wanted to put someone else (me) in their place. It *stung*. It made me question if, because I was only a 1 out of 3, I would ever get to where I wanted to be. It was a setback, but it didn't *stop* me.

Instead, I remember thinking: *Well . . . let's just see how this plays out.* And secretly planning to prove them wrong someday.

That "someday" came two years and two months later.

I had been invited and announced as the mainstage keynote at the National Speakers Association's annual conference. This is one of the highest, most coveted honors of the speaking profession, and presumably only given to "hot speakers" with "hot topics." ;)

The evening before I was scheduled to present, I received an unsolicited email from the person who had sent me the rejection a couple years earlier.

The person wrote:

> *At dinner tonight, a colleague reminded me that I'd rejected you at a local association chapter meeting in 2015 . . . and that you'll be on the main stage tomorrow at the National Speakers Association Conference.*
>
> *Funny how that goes. Looking forward to your talk in the morning!*

Truthfully, by the time I received that follow-up email I had forgotten the original, scathing rejection. My life was chaos trying to manage a speaking career that had suddenly skyrocketed, despite, or perhaps fueled by, rejections like the one they had sent me.

To my rejecter's credit, not many people take the time to acknowledge their "wrongdoing," and a year or so later, a new person in charge of programming at that same local chapter reached out and wondered if I would be able to speak for their spring conference. Unfortunately, I could not—I was booked.

Admittedly the stories don't always tie up so nicely, but sometimes they do. Of course, you'll only notice when that happens if you're paying attention to the story the way a main character would.

Remember this the next time something goes wrong. Something like leaving the office deflated after a day with no progress. Or finding out one of your key players is leaving. Or maybe it's a travel nightmare, like your flight home from the sales conference gets diverted so you miss your connection and end up having to get a room at the airport hotel, which doesn't have room service, so you have to head down to the crummy hotel bar to get a burger.

Right then, repeat to yourself, "Well, let's see how *this* story plays out."

And then don't be surprised when, also stranded and forced to eat a burger at the hotel restaurant, a group of other business travelers and you all end up hanging out together until after the restaurant closes and exchanging information and they become valuable professional contacts, and it all ends happily ever after, after all.

REFRAMING FAILURE

One of the biggest problems facing leaders is that their fear of failure keeps them from taking the necessary risks for new levels of excellence. Research shows that "most leaders are, deep down, afraid of failure."[10]

However, even in the attempts to avoid it, "few careers go unblemished, and big mistakes aren't always terminal."[11] A ten-year study of over 2,600 leaders "showed almost half (45 percent) suffered at least one major career blowup—like getting fired, messing up a major deal, or tanking an acquisition. Despite that, 78 percent of these executives eventually made it to the CEO role."[12]

In fact, Jeff Cohn, a corporate-leadership advisor who helps private-equity firms select executives for portfolio companies, says the firms he advises "actively seek executives who have experienced and—this is the important part—learned from disappointments."[13]

It isn't the failure itself, then, but rather what you *do* with it that matters. And, perhaps more important, what it does to *you*. "Psychologically, it can be the kind of thing that is so devastating that it could rip your entire career apart," says Cohn. "It really does depend on how you deal with it."

Researchers at the Center for Creative Leadership recently conducted a study to determine the difference between a successful executive and one who, as they termed it, "derails."

At first glance, the two groups were indistinguishable. "Both groups (a) were bright and ambitious, (b) had been identified as high potentials early in their careers, (c) had noteworthy records of achievement, and (d) were willing to sacrifice to advance their careers. In addition, both groups possessed very few personal flaws."[14]

The big difference between the two groups? The way they handled mistakes and failures. The "unwillingness or inability to learn from experience appeared to be the major reason the executives derailed."[15]

I'm no fool. I'm pretty sure you already have heard about the importance of learning from failure. Maybe you have a mug with one of a hundred inspirational and aspirational quotes that expresses that kind of sentiment. ("Fall Seven Times and Get Up Eight!" "Failure is a stepping stone to greatness!" "Fail Better!") *And*, I'm pretty sure the derailed executives have *also* heard those quotes and yet, knowing the quote and actually *learning* from failure are two different things.

The problem lies in forgetting our stories of past failures. While the big ones are hard to forget, and certainly not all failures are equal in size, it's the smaller failures that often provide the most value.

Those are the ones that, although things were uncertain and messy at first, you were able to pull through to the other side with minimal damage. Or while errors or poorly managed circumstances led to loss in ground, it wasn't a complete dumpster fire. Or even if it *was* a complete dumpster fire, perhaps it happened long enough ago that the remaining ashes have cleared and a new, more eco-friendly dumpster stands in its place.

Here is the proverbial catch-22 of learning from failures: there's a danger of forgetting that they were ever failures in the first place. After surviving the hard times, you might forget that you ever endured them.

This loss of organizational-failure lore, though common, occurs at the severe detriment to the overall optimism of the team. There is an opportunity for those who refuse to forget these stories, and who actively retell the stories of the times when it felt like "The End" to show there is reason to be optimistic—that things *can* smooth out in time, that they often do, and in such a way that you might forget the bumps were ever there in the first place.

Here's a strategy to help you get better at reframing failure.

STRATEGY #2:
MAKE A LIST OF THE OTHER TIMES
IT FELT LIKE YOU FAILED

Don't worry, this exercise isn't as bad as the title makes it seem. In order to master this Truth, it helps to remember the times, in your past, when it *felt* like the end of the story. When it *felt* like a complete disaster, like everything was coming apart, like you would never recover.

The key word here, is, of course, "felt." And, more particularly, "felt in the moment." Because yes, now looking back with your 20/20 vision, you can see that this "disaster" wasn't the end of the world. Pay attention not to judge who you were in the middle of that story. Having respect and compassion for the person you were in that moment is essential for approaching your current middle with clarity and hope.

Here are a couple of prompts to get you started and an example:

Prompt 1. Write about a time when you felt you were at the end of a story at work (but really it was the middle):

Think back over your career. If you have a hard time "thinking back," jog your memory by scrolling back through your calendar—a couple of weeks, a couple of months, a couple of years—and look at the appointments and projects you were working on.

It might help to get together with a colleague and take a trip down memory lane—not to focus on the great successes (that will come later), but instead to look for those moments of chaos when it felt like it was all coming apart. If you find yourself saying, "Oh my gosh, I totally forgot about that," or "Oh wow! I can't believe we got through that," you're on the right track. The goal is to tap into the part of the story when you *didn't* know how it was going to turn out.

The clearer you get with what happened, how it went wrong, and, most important, how you felt in that middle-of-the-story moment, the better equipped you will be to use that story as a tool for future moments of chaos—a reminder that you've felt this before, this is a middle, this is not the end.

I'll give you a real-life story that I'll call "the DVD debacle."

One executive recalled an experience many years ago when he was responsible for announcing a new sales approach to a large, nation-wide team of salespeople. It was an exciting approach the executive himself had seen in action when he had been pitched by a salesperson from a competing company—a competitor the executive admitted he'd been concerned might steal some of his salespeople. Truthfully, he wouldn't blame them. Their sales strategy had felt stagnant for a while, and this new approach with their own spin on it had the potential to reignite some excitement.

The plan was to send two different DVDs (yes, it was many years ago) to the heads of each regional team—a small but essential group who were fully responsible for rallying the troops around new initiatives. This group had to buy in if the strategy were to ever get off the ground.

The first DVD would reveal the compelling method and reasoning behind this new strategy. Then it would include examples of what the new flow and messaging would look like, using their products and language. And, finally, an exciting projection of what higher rates of closed deals could pencil out to in terms of bonuses and payouts.

The second DVD, to be mailed once the first one was received, would be a direct (bootlegged) copy of the pitch the executive had received from the competitor; the one that was *so irresistible* and inspired the executive to create their own version. By sending *this* DVD, the sales team could see for themselves just how effective the approach could be! The executive and his team prepared the first round of DVDs to be sent. They printed the address labels, stuffed envelopes with the DVDs, and sent the first batch out for delivery.

It wasn't until two days later, when the executive's team started preparing the second mailing, that they uncovered a terrible mistake.

"We sent the wrong DVD!!" the executive exclaimed.

"I was sitting at my desk when one of my staff came in and said, 'Just checking, but wasn't the one with the green font supposed to go first? I think we sent the one with the red font.' And that's when I realized . . . we literally packaged up the best sales pitch I'd ever heard, from the competitor who was already sniffing around my sales team, and sent it straight to *my top people's mailboxes* with *zero* explanation. We didn't even send it with our logo'd envelopes or return addresses or anything. In a matter of hours, they would be opening their mailboxes and putting a DVD in their players with a pitch *so good* I was certain I was going to lose them all."

It was frustrating and terrifying. How could he have messed that up? How big was the fallout going to be? The executive didn't sleep for days as he and the staff scrambled to make it right.

And make it right they did. They put the other DVD—the one that was supposed to go first—in the mail immediately and over-nighted it with a letter that said something like, "You may have received a strange package in the mail the other day," and that if they'd watched that DVD, they were no doubt confused but also intrigued. And that *this* DVD would explain it all.

"It actually ended up working for the better," the executive shared. "Those who watched the wrong DVD first were more invested in the strategy because they didn't *experience* it as a 'strategy' . . . they just experienced it as anyone who was sent that message in that way would."

And then . . . he forgot it ever happened.

All that drama. All that chaos. The stress of not only possibly losing his job over the mistake but also ruining the company—erased entirely. Once the problem was solved, it was all but con-signed to oblivion. When I asked why he thought he had forgotten the incident, he shrugged. "Maybe because it all worked out?"

You likely have many stories over the course of your career that sound similar—and if they ended up working out (which they usually do), you likely forgot them as well. The first prompt will help remind you of the various "failures" you've endured and will build faith that you (and your team) can survive, and even avoid, whatever failures await you.

Prompt 2. Write about a time when you felt you were at the end of a story personally (but really it was the middle):

We've already discussed the power of personal stories in professional leadership, and here is another opportunity to leverage them. Maybe the story is when you faced a health diagnosis or when you were outbid on a real estate deal, or when your partner started a conversation by saying, "Look, we need to talk."

Yes, the stories you find when looking back at your career will be valuable both for you *and* for the team members with whom you share them. Organizational narratives told to draw attention to the middle, as the research discussed earlier in the chapter, help the collective effort to make sense of the story currently lived based on clues from stories in the past.

However, do not limit yourself by omitting *personal* stories. The stories of the middles you've endured outside of the office can also have a powerful impact on how you approach the middles at work.

A few areas rich in content can include:

- Any competitive environments (games, tournaments, matches)

- Any big decisions (education, moves, family)

- Health (illness, treatment, recovery)

- Financial uncertainty or hardship (unexpected unemployment, bankruptcy, the market)

Certainly personal reflection is fertile ground for growth of any kind; however, in this case you are looking specifically for instances when you thought it was over or ending, but in reality, you were in the middle. Focus your attention there first—how challenging it was, why you made the decisions you did, how you felt, and how long you were able to endure. Only after there is a fullness to that part of the recollection should you revisit how it all turned out. This exercise will remind you not only of your strength as a leader but of your essence as a *person*. Use these stories as powerful reminders the next time you find yourself faced with a challenge—a reminder that though things don't look great now, you just never know what might happen next.

SPECTACULAR FAILURE OR SPECTACULAR FUTURE?

On April 20, 2023, just six years after the *New York Times* article about Tesla and Musk's penchant for story, another Musk company, SpaceX, launched a Starship rocket test launch. The rocket spent approximately four minutes in the air before experiencing a "rapid unscheduled disassembly"[16]—or, in other words, it blew up in spectacular fashion. (Though, yes, from now on anytime something in my life doesn't go as planned, you better believe I'm going to call it "rapid unscheduled disassembly," and I hope you will do the same.)

Since the perfect result of the launch[17] would have included ninety minutes of airtime and a controlled landing of the estimated $2–3 billion rocket[18] in the ocean near Hawaii, many were surprised to hear that Musk was thrilled.

Watching the video of the launch, you can hear the gasps as the ship began to spin and eventually erupt into a massive fireball—and as it did, the control room erupted into uproarious applause. Multiple headlines referred to Musk popping bottles of champagne with his team, and the man himself tweeted: "Congrats SpaceX team on an exciting test launch of Starship! Learned a lot for next test launch in a few months."[19]

Their spaceship exploded. It lasted four minutes instead of ninety, and still they cheered.

Think about that for a moment. Do you think that would be the same reaction from previous organizations who have pursued space exploration—cheers upon explosion instead of years of finger-pointing and bureaucratic drama? Or think about the organizations and leaders you've worked for who put everything on the line. Can you imagine if, when the efforts resulted in complete and public obliteration, the first *instinct*, without hesitation . . . was to celebrate? It seems laughable. And yet, incredible innovation is possible when a leader understands that rapid unscheduled disassembly is part of a greater story.

Much was written following the unplanned obliteration of Elon Musk's SpaceX rocket in April 2023. Not only about the explosion, but the other risks that Musk was taking. One commentator pointed out that in the span of twenty-four hours, Elon Musk had made three very big bets with three separate companies: Twitter, Tesla, and SpaceX.

And while the only thing I know for sure is that no one—not even Musk himself—has any idea how these companies and risks will have panned out by the time you're reading the words on this page, a few quotes stood out, including: "Mr. Musk's most important contribution would be his powerful attitude to risk,"[20] and a social post stating: "When you set up each initiative as a learning experiment (and of course, have raised the sources to do so!) you essentially extend the frontiers of knowledge and progress."[21]

Mistakes happen. Unexpected obstacles appear. Blind spots reveal themselves too late. Misjudgments, miscalculations, and misunderstandings are more common than not. These things are inevitable, and they are also *important* because they will happen again. What separates the best from the legendary are those individuals who, when facing the chaos, can remind themselves that this is the middle, not the end. Whether your goal is to get to Mars or to Carnegie Hall or to a stage in an arena filled with listeners or to the highest rank in your company's hierarchy or something else entirely . . . there are going to be middles of the story that look a lot like explosions (for my *Stories That Stick* readers, I hope you're smiling). The best leaders can recognize the story while it's happening and create a culture that is free to live and work and explore doing the same.

Each time things go wrong, a story is born, one that is much sweeter when things eventually go right. This might feel like a failure now, but the story is not over yet. Use the professional and personal stories from this exercise to remind yourself that, just like all the middles you have faced before, this ending is yet to be written.

And won't it be exciting to see how it all turns out?

That is optimism in action.

ELEVEN

A Roadmap for Resilience

"It is your reaction to adversity, not the adversity itself,
that determines how your life's story will develop."

—DIETER F. UCHTDORF

Have you ever read the fable called "The Fern and the Bamboo"? It tells the story of a carpenter whose success is upended when a furniture company moves into his town, creating better and cheaper pieces than the carpenter can construct. His finances plunge. The stress affects his marriage. His children begin to fail in school. He becomes truly desperate.

One day, he goes on a walk in a nearby forest to clear his mind. Deep in the woods, he meets a kind old man who invites him to his home for tea and conversation. The carpenter shares the stories of his misfortunes with the stranger. When they are done with their tea, the old man invites the carpenter to walk on the land behind his house, and there he points to a grove of soaring bamboo with lush green ferns growing all around.

The old man tells the carpenter that he planted the ferns and the bamboo at the same time, eight years before.

"I put all my effort in taking care of them, as though they were a treasure," he says.

He then tells the carpenter that in just a few months, the fern had grown beautiful and strong, while the bamboo seeds remained under the ground, seemingly lifeless.

After a year, the fern kept growing, but there was still no sign of the bamboo.

Another year passed with the same results: glorious ferns and no bamboo.

Finally, after five years, the old man says, twigs began to appear at the site where he'd planted the bamboo.

After a few months, though it felt like overnight, the bamboo grew tall and strong. They towered over the ferns like skyscrapers, leaving not even a hint that at one point it was ever a question of which would be the more dominant, abundant plant.

The carpenter and old man admire the majestic bamboo forest in front of them.

"Do you know why it took so long to grow?" the old man asks. The carpenter remains silent.

"It took five years for the bamboo to grow because the plant was working on taking root from the ground," he says. "It knew that in order for it to grow very tall, it needed a firm base before coming out of the ground."

The old man further explains: "Sometimes things take time because they are taking root. You must persist and not lose faith."

There's a lot to unpack in that one simple story. Patience. Comparison. Perhaps most important, not giving up even when progress is slow and a goal seems frustratingly out of reach. Especially if you know there is potential and have a sense for what is possible. All these unpleasantries can be wrapped up in one big goal: resilience.

RESILIENCE:
A MUSCLE THAT CAN BE BUILT

According to the American Psychological Association, resilience is "the process and outcome of successfully adapting to difficult or challenging life experiences, especially through mental, emotional, and behavioral flexibility and adjustment to external and internal demands."[1]

I'll put that a bit more simply: resilience is the ability to bounce back after tough times, recover from setbacks, and deal with challenges in a positive way. There are so many great setback-to-success stories. You know that basketball great Michael Jordan was cut from his high school basketball team and was told, when he was in college, that he wasn't good enough to play professionally. Or Oprah Winfrey's rags-to-riches story of being born into poverty and suffering every kind of abuse as a child, and then going on to be the country's first Black female billionaire. Stories like these and the many others you've heard require, perhaps above all, resilience.

And when it comes to this essential leadership quality, there is good news. In the book *Option B: Facing Adversity, Building Resilience, and Finding Joy*, tech executive and philanthropist Sheryl

Sandberg describes how her friend (and coauthor), psychologist Adam Grant, told her there are concrete things people can do to recover from life-shattering events.

Resilience, he told her, is a muscle that can be built.[2]

How does this relate to the Story Edge truth that you are always in the middle of a story?

Well, imagine if Michael Jordan, on his college team, was discouraged and opted to quit the sport because he wasn't yet a pro ball player instead of being cognizant of *how far he'd come* since his high school days? He was in the middle of his story.

Or if Oprah, as a young journalist, had allowed herself to give up her larger dreams of creating a media empire, thinking she was at the pinnacle of her career as a local news broadcaster, instead of recognizing *how far she had come* since her first, early setbacks? She was in the middle of her story.

Both Jordan and Winfrey (and countless other highly successful people) didn't let themselves get stuck or locked in a false narrative, but instead kept building those resilience muscles, knowing there was more to come.

At any given point on any team or leader's path to the goals they seek, it may feel like it's taking longer than it should. That the cards are stacked too high against us. That the odds are never in our favor. It is these moments that resilience is built, and knowing you are in the middle of a story helps put the path to success in perspective.

Though you aren't where you want to be, remember that you are further along than when you started.

IN ORDER TO KEEP GOING . . .
LOOK HOW FAR YOU'VE COME

It was the early 2010s and for one of the thirty major league baseball teams, it was a historic season. For the first time in decades, the team was heading to the playoffs and word on the street was they had all the makings of a World Series champion. Unfortunately, the team wasn't able to live up to the hype and instead lost before making it to the final games. And while many of the team's superfans joked that the World Series was canceled that year, the team's management decided to take the opportunity to up their internal game and brought on a man we'll call Alan Michaels as their new executive vice president.

Alan Michaels is an analytics guy. He always has been. He'll even tell you he met his wife in college when they bonded over their shared love of Excel spreadsheets. So, it shouldn't have come as a surprise when, after his success as senior VP of Strategy and Business Analytics for a different major league team, Alan was recruited to replicate the same success.

However, despite being one of the most beloved brands in all of baseball (or maybe because of it), behind the scenes of the team's big baseball diamond was a mere handful of committed people making things happen.

In an interview with Michaels, he recalled those early days with his new franchise. "I remember some of my early meetings with the team and asking, 'Who's in charge of the social media accounts?' and the team looked at me and said, 'No one.' And social media was definitely 'a thing' at this point. They looked at my face and could tell maybe that wasn't the right answer so added that they had someone, but he left seven months ago. And I'm thinking . . . you have

2 million Twitter followers! I'm following all of your accounts and you're posting stuff every day . . . someone has to be doing it. 'Who does that?' And they said, 'Oh, we, we just gave it to an intern.'"

The same was true for customer service; one woman was responsible for answering (or not answering) thousands of emails.

And the same was true for ticket sales.

"Baseball is very much about nightly ticket sales," Alan told me. Fortunately, people were buying tickets; that wasn't the issue. But the *tracking* of the ticket-buying was less of a science and more of an elevated guessing game. Ticket-sale updates came from the ticketing office in an email with a few numbers typed into it. And though the seats weren't empty, without any data or analytics in place, they were pretty much relying on the "if you build it, they will come" strategy. It was time for an upgrade, and Alan was the man for the job, if for no other reason than he understood that data architecture, much like Rome, isn't built in a day.

And it all started with his beloved spreadsheets.

"There are business intelligence tools, like Tableau, that are really valuable. But if you just put Tableau on top of old spreadsheets . . ." Alan laughed as he said it (as only a person who truly loves spreadsheets would), ". . . it's just a better-looking spreadsheet."

Alan was curious and had questions: *What were the dashboards built on? What's the data warehouse structure? Who manages the data architecture? The databases where the numbers are pulled from—are they automated, not automated, who's updating them?*

In order to achieve what they were looking to achieve, it was going to take more than a few spreadsheets. It was going to take people. *Good* people.

"We needed to go through the process of getting people—to create an entire department, bring in the right skill sets and backgrounds." They needed to hire a head of strategy analytics who would then go through the process of getting to know the landscape, IT, and data infrastructure in order to make assessments and suggest what was possible and how many people it would take. And then there was the actual construction, implementation, and finally full incorporation of the new employees and systems at all levels of the organization. All of this while *also* being sensitive that the current, extremely dedicated team didn't feel threatened.

"The whole process takes time," Alan explained calmly, matter-of-factly, and without a hint of the subtext that permeates so many big undertakings. He didn't give the heavy "time is a necessary evil" sigh or speak with the subtle "the process takes time, but we don't have any time so it's better if it *doesn't* take time" anxious tone. A seasoned, resilient, Story Forward Leader already, he was comfortable with the fact that time was required. More important, Alan knew what would be required of *him,* the leader, as progress was slowly made and the time slowly passed: he'd need to tell them stories of how far they'd come.

The day the owners of the team were frustrated that everything still felt upside-down, Alan was able to remind them of how the operations were becoming standardized, streamlined, and profitable. He could tell the story of the once haphazard social media strategy and show them how their platform was growing, resulting in higher ticket sales that, now that this office was being run well, could be tracked and mined for information on their customers.

"Anytime you come to an organization or you're in an organization that's looking to make big changes, the most important thing a leader can do is tell the team the stories of how far you've come," Alan said. "Because yeah, it can be discouraging, it can feel frustrating, and it's the leader's job to reorient the thinking from just: 'Look how far we have left to go,' to 'Look how far we've come.'"

Operation Analytics (my name for it, not his) took Alan and his team about three years. Three years to fully adopt, develop, adjust, and integrate before the initiative was fully implemented.

"It's not that we weren't doing anything," Alan said. "It's that it takes time." It took time to do the obvious things like assess and hire and build. "*And* it took time to manage change and the effectiveness of change and the buy-in to change so that we could have a well-functioning team."

But what a difference the three years made.

Not unlike the bamboo in the fable, at the end of it, "We had an automated dashboard that shows our ticket sales on a daily basis, and it's accurate. Our finance team believes it's accurate. Our sales team believes it's accurate and they rely on it," Alan said. "I could walk into the office and pull up an interactive dashboard to identify trends and catch issues before they became problems—a very different experience from getting an email from the ticketing people with a few numbers copied and pasted into it."

Alan knew the transformation was complete when people weren't just asking questions about the data, but when they were *using* data language to make decisions.

"They would say something like, 'Hey, I noticed something was interesting on Tuesday nights or Wednesday nights—there was a dip or there was an increase' . . . The conversations were *different*. Instead of approaching problems just frustrated that we didn't have X, Y, or Z . . . they were using the tools and solving problems in an energetic and excited way . . . using what they had to build something even better."

When Alan eventually left that team, real transformation had taken place, thanks to his patience and strategic work. And he had plenty of stories to tell, to remind the team just how far they'd come.

The truth is, as humans—especially as motivated, success-seeking humans—we suffer from what I call "story amnesia." We lose track of the progress we've made because we're just too focused on the quest for more progress to revisit where we've been. Alan knew this, and it's important that you know it too.

In his book *Be Your Future Self Now,* author Dr. Benjamin Hardy points out, "If a stranger could have a conversation with the person you were 10 years ago, and the person you are today, they'd be talking to two totally different people."[3]

He, as you may have guessed by the title of his book, used this statement to make the point that your ten-year Future-Self will be just as different from your Today-Self, as your Today-Self is from the ten-years-ago you.

However, it also speaks to the fact that we often *forget*, or at least lose track of, how much *better* we are now, how much further along, than we were in the past. A Story Forward Leader harnesses the power of these stories by knowing that though it may feel like you've barely gotten started, you are *not* at the beginning of your story. You have already come so far. You are in the middle.

Here's another strategy to help build your resilience muscle through stories.

STRATEGY #3:
REVISIT YOUR OWN STORYLINE TO
FIND FORGOTTEN BEGINNINGS

Have you ever heard the metaphor about boiling a frog? That a frog can be thrown in a pot of tepid water and not notice as the temperature is raised slowly to a boil? The frog doesn't register the heat until the water is boiling, and then it is too late for him to survive. The story is meant to warn us of the dangers of "creeping normality," that slow change can be dangerous, and you might not even realize it's happening . . . until it's too late.

But creeping normality doesn't always mean harm in the traditional sense; it can also mean the slow, subtle amnesia that accompanies *progress*. Our tendency to forget the temperature of the water at the start once the temperature has moved. What was once warm is now chilly, what was once a pipe dream is now a memory.

No, it's not visually as grotesque as the slow, unsuspecting death of an innocent amphibian, but it is equally as tragic. Losing touch *with how far we've come* disconnects us from our own resilience and eventually leads to the kind of caution and rigidity that have left far more careers short of their potential than metaphoric frogs on stovetops.

Remember, you are not a cat . . . don't be a frog either.

Much like the strategy in the previous chapter, this strategy requires you to take a trip down memory lane. However, this time, instead of looking for times when you were in the middle of the story but thought you were at the end, your task is to look for various *beginnings*.

Ask yourself the following questions and consider jotting down your answers.

1. How many people were on your team when you first started? If it's grown, take a moment to reflect on that (especially if it's grown a lot).

2. What were a few of the earliest goals you and your team were shooting for? If the goal is bigger, take a moment to reflect on how far you've come.

3. What was one of the first big deals you closed—how much was it for? How does that compare to the deals you're closing now?

4. Who was your first boss? What did you notice about this person? Was that person a model to you, or did you want to do things differently than they did?

5. When is a moment when you truly felt hopeful about a big project, when you knew things would likely turn out great?

After you've done this for yourself and your own career and progress, as a leader, I invite you to do it again for your team—both as individuals and as the collective group. Finally, just like you read in Alan's story (and even mentioned in Truth 2), tell these stories to your *team* so they can see how far you *all* have come and, in doing so, inspire belief in their own resilience.

AGILITY TO GAIN RESILIENCE

I decided to start running. Again. I do this often. One might suggest I don't *stop* running so I don't have to keep *starting* again, but alas . . . that is a discussion for a different time.

One chilly, late-winter morning, I was running on the dirt path that traverses through Central Park. I prefer that path to the road because it's wider, less crowded, and gives me more space to do my thing.

So, imagine my surprise when, out of the corner of my eye, I saw something approaching my left shoulder from behind. By the time I turned, a guy ran past me within just a few inches. I was a little annoyed at first, and then indignant. *Who did he think he was?!* And what would have happened if, right at that moment, I had decided to dodge one of the puddles that peppered the dirt path and ran right into him?

I kept my eye on him (he was admittedly hard to miss in his fluorescent orange tights) as he ran ahead of me, and I found my annoyance melt into awe. The way that man could zig around puddles and zag around poodles. He dodged and darted with such ease, such nimbleness. He could come to a complete stop, change direction, pivot out of the way, and get moving again all within the blink of an eye.

That's why he passed so closely to me—because he *could*. He knew that even if I made a sudden move, he'd have the *agility* to change course.

This shouldn't have come as a surprise to me. Agility has long been a secret edge in athletics. Hall of Fame football players Lynn Swann and Herschel Walker took ballet classes. More recently, defensive tackle Steve McLendon discussed taking ballet as a means to staying injury free. "It keeps . . . your ankles, keeps your feet strong, your toes strong, you get away from knee injuries," McLendon said.[4]

Agility is essential in business too. An agile business can rapidly recognize and adapt to changing circumstances to protect its stakeholders' interests. Similarly, agile leaders possess the ability to adjust and redirect their teams when their business's operating environment and priorities shift, simultaneously preserving a positive social dynamic and creating more efficient business outcomes.

In a survey of 130 senior executives and human resource professionals in the Fortune 500, the executives stated that "agility is one of the most critical leadership capacities needed in their companies today." That quote likely doesn't surprise you. The fact that the article was published in 2007 might. It turns out that being able to lead effectively, even (or especially) in times of rapid change and high complexity, has been a priority for more than a decade.[5]

Organizational experts have been calling for the need to develop more agile organizations, and yet there is still much progress to be made. What is responsible for this ongoing "agility gap"?

The lack of agile leaders.

"To develop teams and organizations with the level of agility demanded by today's turbulent business environment, companies need leaders who embody a corresponding level of agility."[6] According to experts, agility requires intention and a willingness to become uncomfortable. Agile leaders are committed to remaining open-minded to new processes, ideas, and solutions and avoiding the tendency to default to doing things the way they've been done in the past.[7]

Most important, agility requires not only a clear vision of where you are going but the strength and flexibility to not get stuck in the puddles or spooked by the poodles that might block your planned course. It requires that you remain mindful that you're always in the middle of a story so you can stay loose and disconnected from obsessing over an outcome.

STRATEGY #4:
DISCONNECT FROM THE OUTCOME

Since we started this chapter with a parable, I thought I'd give you another. This one is ancient; it likely originates from an early Han Dynasty Chinese essay collection called the *Huainanzi* and is frequently referred to as "Sài Wēng Shī Mǎ," which translates to "The Old Man on the Frontier Lost (His) Horse."

The story goes that once there was a farmer who lived with his father. One day, unprovoked and through no fault of his own, the farmer's horse ran away. With a significant part of this family's wealth now missing, the people came to commiserate.

"We are so sorry you lost your horse. What an unfortunate thing to have happen."

The farmer's father responded, "We shall see."

Several months later, the farmer's horse returned, but not alone. The horse had returned with seven wild horses, significantly increasing the farmer and his father's wealth. Everyone in town congratulated him. *What great fortune!*

But his father whispered, "We shall see."

The following day, the farmer tried to ride one of the wild horses. However, the farmer fell from the horse and broke his leg.

The people lamented, "Oh, how terrible!"

The farmer's father responded, "We shall see."

Not long after, barbarians invaded the territory where the farmer and his father lived, and all of the young men of the village were to report to battle. The farmer, however, could not, for his leg still hadn't healed. Most of the men were killed but the farmer and his father were spared.

The lesson is equal parts simple and profound. Good luck can bring about misfortune, misfortune can be transformed into a blessing, a blessing can become a curse . . . and the story continues. The secret to agility and resilience lies here—in the ability to practice patience and discipline in the suspension between where you think you are in the story and what you think that means.

You are always on this story continuum and, therefore, always in the middle.

Next time a great stroke of fortune—or misfortune—comes your way, try whispering, "We shall see."

AND THEY ALL
LIVED HAPPILY EVER AFTER.
THE ~~END~~ MIDDLE.

Though I never played an organized sport, I am grateful for sports seasons. Grateful for the journey they take us on, for the wrap-up at the end even when my team didn't win, for the break during the offseason (yes, even as a fan), and then for the season to start back up again—new, fresh, the beginning. And on the days when I feel like I've endured enough uncertainty, movies about sports are even better because they, without fail, follow the perfect story arc: team players struggle, a leader emerges, they work hard together, they win the championship, the credits roll, The (satisfying) End!

And then one night my family, after a significant amount of arguing, all agreed on watching the Disney+ movie *Chang Can Dunk*. In the movie, Chang is a high school band student and basketball enthusiast who has an intense rivalry with his former elementary school friend Matt, a popular basketball star on their school's team. The boys go head-to-head in several adolescent face-offs, and as the tension between them reaches its peak, the boys make a bet.

It hinges on a single question:

Can Chang make a dunk on the basketball court by homecoming?

They wager a cherished Pokémon trading card and a Kobe Bryant jersey and agree that the loser will also face the humiliation of shaving his head.

Desperate to dunk the ball despite his underwhelming five-foot-eight stature, Chang enlists the help of a dunking mentor, Deandre, and the two document his reinvention on Deandre's YouTube channel. Insert standard movie montage of master and student, except in this story—despite his progress—the night before the public dunk challenge, Chang is overwhelmed by the pressure, and in the dark of night, mysteriously sneaks into the school's gymnasium where the contest will take place.

The next morning, Chang makes the dunk and achieves instant notoriety, even gaining the attention of ESPN. But questions arise when Chang is unable to duplicate the dunk, and eventually the truth comes out: Chang cheated. During his late-night trip to the court, he lowered the basketball hoop and fooled the world.

Much to my family's frustration, I quickly paused the film on several occasions to see how much time remained. How were they going to redeem the cheater with so few minutes left? Yes, the whole movie was about a kid learning to dunk, but I was genuinely concerned that he was running out of time—even in the movie world.

As the last few minutes of the movie play, we see Chang make the team, we see him playing in a game, we see him running toward the basket, leaping through the air, hand high over his head, ball in dunking position, mouth stretched open and wide, and then . . . it's over.

The movie ends without us actually seeing Chang dunk.

Without us knowing if he does.

Or even can.

And I loved it!

It was the best sports movie I've ever seen (yes, I'm including *The Sandlot* here, and, no, *Ted Lasso* is not a movie). Why do I love it so much? Because whether Chang could or couldn't dunk that day is not the end of the story. Yes, the script was done and the credits rolled. But ending it in that way made it feel as if the story kept going.

The same is true for us. We can't turn our lives off. They keep going until we take our last breath (and even then, they go on in the stories others tell about us, but that is a discussion for a different time).

This is not to abandon reality—the deal might well be falling apart, the market might well be crashing, circumstances both in and out of your control may be stacking against you with increasing speed like the cubes of a Tetris game, and there seems to be no way to complete the round successfully and advance to the next level. Failure may be imminent, or things might just be kind of bad for a while. Either way, how a leader handles it psychologically truly matters.

It helps to remember that, by nature, middles are messy. Middles are hard. They're filled with uncertainty, confusing, and full of conflict. Middles can feel unfair. You might feel frustrated or wronged and be fully justified in both. It's not you. That is just how middles are. And in recognizing that, in trusting it, you free yourself just a little bit. Eventually, over time, the story plays out. In hindsight, the events will no longer be random acts of devastation but stepping stones that either brought you closer to your goals or taught you lessons you needed to learn until you reached an ending you're satisfied with.

The story doesn't end—it continues.

The Infinity Edge

"Carve your name on hearts, not tombstones.
A legacy is etched into the minds of others
and the stories they share about you."

—SHANNON ALDER

H ave you ever seen the Broadway musical *Rent*?
Even if you haven't, you might be familiar with its most famous song: "Seasons of Love."

It begins:

Five hundred twenty-five thousand, six hundred minutes
Five hundred twenty-five thousand moments so dear
Five hundred twenty-five thousand, six hundred minutes
How do you measure, measure a year?
In daylights, in sunsets
In midnights, in cups of coffee
In inches, in miles
In laughter, in strife

In five hundred twenty-five thousand, six hundred minutes
How do you measure, a year in the life?

The song speaks to legacy. What do we want to leave behind? What stories do we want others to tell about us?

It speaks to the passage of time. How many minutes do we have over the course of our lives? How do we want to spend them?

What is the *impact* we can make in the "five hundred twenty-five thousand, six hundred minutes" that make up a common year?

Impact is hard to measure.

Reading about the Cuban Missile Crisis, knowing little more about JFK than he was the youngest to ever be elected president, he was assassinated, he likely had a thing with Marilyn Monroe, and what the cologne he wore smelled like (which is a great story) . . . I found myself wishing he had been around longer, had another few years, at least, to create his legacy. That he had had more time to lead. He had served just over one thousand days, a mere third of what could have been possible.

I was talking to a colleague who shared a similar sentiment about Kobe Bryant. My colleague was a Celtics fan and strongly disliked Kobe on the basketball court.

"But when we learned what kind of man, what kind of leader he was," my colleague said, "it's no surprise that it seemed the country stopped, or at least paused briefly, in shock and deep sadness—a sadness that initially surprised those non-Laker fans and even more so, the non-basketball fans. That January day when news of the helicopter crash spread . . . millions mourned the loss, not of a great player, but a great leader. Not just a great leader at his job . . . but a great leader as a human."

This is possible for each of us. To leave a legacy. To make an impact. To leave stories behind, of living with purpose, of living authentically, of being a person who includes rather than excludes, who judges a book not by its cover but by the power of the story it tells.

To take the time and have the courage to *seek out* the rest of the story—to give others the respect of knowing them better. To commit to *telling* our stories, so that people may have more opportunity to connect, to see things more clearly. And to always remember that even in our most difficult moments, we are in the middle of a story, a story that is being written, and though it may not make sense right now, it is a story we can someday tell.

It is through our stories that we, as leaders, as *people,* are remembered. And as long as our story is told, we live on. Which is . . . the *ultimate* edge.

THE *INFINITY* STORY EDGE

Many years ago, I was trying to make a quick run to the coffee shop before picking my kids up from preschool. I was already running a little late so the coffee stop was ambitious, but nevertheless, I was going for it.

As I came to an intersection the light turned green (yay!), and I was just about to go when a cop pulled right in front of my car and stopped traffic for a funeral procession. *Oh no*, I thought. Oh no as in—it was terrible someone passed away, *and* Oh no as in—now I was *definitely* going to be late for preschool pickup.

I had barely finished that thought when . . . the procession was over.

I mean it seriously couldn't have been more than six cars.

The cop left.

The intersection cleared.

And we were free to go.

Except I didn't.

I sat frozen in place. The guy behind me had to honk because I was so lost in thought.

You see, earlier that day, a friend and fellow business owner had said to me, "I don't tell stories because I don't have any."

She didn't seek stories because she didn't expect to find any there.

She didn't tell stories because she thought no one would want, much less need, to hear them.

She didn't consider that her life *was, is, and always will be* a collision of a million little stories, paths taken, decisions made . . . a constant unfolding story.

And that's when I realized, sitting at the intersection, the two could be connected—my "story-less" friend and the way-too-short funeral procession.

Of course, there are many reasons a funeral procession might be short (weather, at the top of the list), but on my mind that day was this:

In the end, it really does come down to impact. How we *impact* the people around us. Do we make a difference in their lives— influence behaviors that make things better? Do people learn from us? And are we curious enough to learn from them? Do we add value or perspective? Do we help them see the value *they* bring . . . simply by living their own unfolding story and intersecting it with our own?

This is my deepest hope and belief of what's possible for you—the Story Forward . . .

That when it is your last day above ground, I have no doubt the room will be filled with people and that it will be *so loud* because everyone will be sharing the stories you once shared with them. They'll tell the stories of the stories they told *you*—because you always wanted to hear them. And they'll tell the stories that you created together, messy middles and all. Big or small, there will be endless stories of the way you made a difference in their professional and personal lives.

What more could we ask for from a leader?

What more could we hope for *as* a leader?

I hope when it is *your* procession going by that there's an impatient person sitting at the stoplight, and they have to wait for *so long* that they are forced to ask themselves, *Who was that?* and *What kind of a person was so worthy to make such a difference?*

All because you had the wisdom to know there is always a story and to take the time to hear it.

That you had the courage to tell your stories—big or small—to influence and inspire others and remind them that they matter.

And that even in the face of the most difficult challenges . . . you helped others to remember that we're always in the middle of the story that is being written right now.

That is how you leave a legacy.

That is how you live forever.

That is the ultimate Story Edge.

APPENDIX

The Story of Rocky the Raccoon

(See Chapter 1)

Once upon a time, in a dense forest, there lived a raccoon named Rocky. Rocky had always felt different from the other animals in the forest. He didn't climb trees or forage for food like the other raccoons. Instead, he spent his days observing the humans who lived in the nearby town. He was fascinated by their clothes, their houses, and the way they walked on two legs.

One day, while wandering through the forest, Rocky came across a discarded pair of pants and a shirt. He picked them up and put them on, feeling a sense of excitement and belonging as he did so. From that day on, he made it his mission to become more human-like.

Rocky started to walk on two legs, just like the humans he had seen. He practiced speaking, mimicking the words he heard the humans say. He even built himself a little house, using branches and leaves to mimic the houses he had seen in the town.

As time passed, Rocky became more and more convinced that he was, in fact, a human. He spent his days exploring the town, observing the humans, and trying to fit in. He was careful to stay out of sight, knowing that the other animals would not understand his desire to be human.

One day, Rocky was discovered by a group of humans. They were shocked to see a raccoon wearing clothes and walking on two legs. They captured him and brought him to a wildlife sanctuary, where he was placed in a cage with other raccoons.

Rocky was heartbroken. He had finally found where he belonged, only to have it taken away from him. He realized that no matter how much he wanted it, he could never truly be human. He belonged in the wild, with his own kind.

Rocky spent the rest of his days in the sanctuary, but he never forgot his dream of being human. He passed on his knowledge to the other raccoons, teaching them to walk on two legs and speak, in the hope that one day they too could experience the thrill of feeling human.

Rocky's story serves as a reminder that we should all be content with who we are and not strive to be someone else. We are all unique and special in our own way.

ACKNOWLEDGMENTS

Of the three books I've written thus far, this one was the most challenging. It took the most time with the slowest perceived progress. Fortunately, I have an incredible group of people cheering me on and a great team who make it all come together.

When I think back on my time as an author, the woman who has been there from the beginning is my agent, Kathy Schneider. If ever I need a good laugh or a good cry, Kathy is there. Thank you for everything you and the team at JRA does—including Tori Clayton, who works to make sure these words are read around the world.

The hardest part of writing a book is getting started. I've always worked best by establishing an outline and then going from there. But sometimes even the outline is tough. That's where Dan Clements comes in. Thank you for sitting with me in that first frustrating phase of figuring out what this book was even about! I am also grateful for Jennifer Grant, who helped clean up and sort through and slow down some of my thoughts. Thank you for the sanity you brought at the time I needed it most. The words on these pages are better because of you.

A big thank-you to my editor, Tim Burgard, for all of the conversations and iterations of direction. Your guidance and patience are invaluable. And of course, to the team at HarperCollins Leadership, without whom these words wouldn't be printed on a page and the books wouldn't be on the shelves.

To my VA, Tori Clark, thank you for the endless hours of research and answering random requests. You are better than AI could ever hope to be (and you can tell your mom I'm not paid to say that). And thank you to my team member Andrea, who ensures that I'm still presenting on stages even in the midst of writing season.

To my friends and followers on social media and my dedicated readers—thank you for coming along with me on the wild ride for each book. Your stories of the impact of stories are what I live for!

Finally, to my family, Michael and my sweet kiddos. From the deepest part of my heart, thank you. I know book season isn't easy. It's hard when I'm away writing (and it's hard when I'm home wor-rying about writing too!). These books are possible because of your generosity and love.

NOTES

Introduction

1. Yuval Noah Harari, *Sapiens: A Brief History of Humankind* (New York: Harper, 2015).
2. Harari, *Sapiens*, 19.
3. Ken Baskin, "Storied Spaces: The Human Equivalent of Complex Adaptive Systems," *Emergence: Complexity & Organization* 10, no. 2 (2008): 19.
4. Baskin, "Storied Spaces," 25.
5. Harari, *Sapiens*, 33.
6. Harari, *Sapiens*, 34.

Chapter One

1. Charles Mackay, *Extraordinary Popular Delusions and the Madness of Crowds* (Boston: L. C. Page & Co., 1932), 89–92.
2. Mackay, *Extraordinary Popular Delusions and the Madness of Crowds*, 89–92.
3. Gary Burnison, "Seeing Stars," Insights blog, Korn Ferry, https://www.kornferry.com/insights/special-edition/seeing-stars.
4. Kevin Roose, "The Brilliance and Weirdness of ChatGPT," *New York Times*, December 5, 2022, https://www.nytimes.com/2022/12/05/technology/chatgpt-ai-twitter.html.
5. Aaron Mok and Jacob Zinkula, "ChatGPT May Be Coming For Our Jobs. Here Are the 10 Roles that AI Is Most Likely to Replace," *Business Insider*, updated September 4, 2023, https://www.businessinsider.com/chatgpt-jobs-at-risk-replacement-artificial-intelligence-ai-labor-trends-2023-02.
6. Kate Murphy, "What We Lose When Companies Make Things Easier for Consumers," *Wall Street Journal*, November 18, 2022, https://www.wsj.com/articles/companies-frictionless-consumers-loss-11668721344.

7. Murphy, "What We Lose When Companies Make Things Easier for Consumers."
8. David Sax, "Why Strangers Are Good For Us," *New York Times*, June 12, 2022, https://www.nytimes.com/2022/06/12/opinion/strangers-talking-benefits.html.
9. Sax, "Why Strangers Are Good for Us."
10. "Facebook's New Motto: 'Move Fast And Please Please Please Don't Break Anything,'" *Halting Problem*, May 21, 2017, https://medium.com/halting-problem/facebooks-new-motto-move-fast-and-please-please-please-don-t-break-anything-8aefdd405d15.
11. Suzy Welch, "Generation Z Yearns for Stability," *Wall Street Journal*, March 22, 2023, https://www.wsj.com/articles/generation-z-yearns-for-stability-workforce-job-market-financial-crisis-hard-work-burnout-self-care-nyu-college-student-fa56b35f.
12. Mackay, *Extraordinary Popular Delusions and the Madness of Crowds*, xiii.

Chapter Two

1. Karina Hof, "What's in a Meme? The Uncanny Journey of 'But First, Coffee,'" Sprudge.com, December 18, 2017, https://sprudge.com/but-first-coffee-128580.html.
2. Timothy J. McClimon, "CEOs' Most Important Business Challenges in 2022," *Forbes*, January 27, 2022, https://www.forbes.com/sites/timothyjmcclimon/2022/01/27/ceos-most-important-business-challenges-in-2022/.
3. Forbes Coaches Council, "Faced Big Challenges in 2022? 15 Ways CEOs Can Rally the Team for the New Year," *Forbes*, January 3, 2022, https://www.forbes.com/sites/forbescoachescouncil/2023/01/03/faced-big-challenges-in-2022-15-ways-ceos-can-rally-the-team-for-the-new-year/?sh=31aa2ca11ac3.
4. James B. Stewart, "Tesla Has Something Hotter Than Cars to Sell: Its Story," *New York Times*, April 6, 2017, https://www.nytimes.com/2017/04/06/business/tesla-story-stocks.html.
5. Ron Lieber, "How Charlie Javice Got JPMorgan to Pay $175 Million for . . . What Exactly?" *New York Times*, January 21, 2023, https://www.nytimes.com/2023/01/21/business/jpmorgan-chase-charlie-javice-fraud.html.
6. Naomi Elegant, "This Wharton Alum's Startup Helps College Students Negotiate Their Financial Aid Packages," *The Daily Pennsylvanian*, January 17, 2018, https://www.thedp.com/article/2018/01/frank-financial-aid-wharton-upenn-penn-philadelphia-startup.
7. Lieber, "How Charlie Javice Got JPMorgan to Pay $175 Million."
8. Lieber, "How Charlie Javice Got JPMorgan to Pay $175 Million."

Chapter Three

1. Sheldon M. Stern, "The Inside Story of the Cuban Missile Crisis," *Boston Globe*, October 6, 2002, http://archive.boston.com/news/globe/magazine/articles /2002/10/06/the_inside_story_of_the_cuban_missile_crisis.
2. University of Virginia Miller Center, https://millercenter.org/the-presidency /secret-white-house-tapes/meeting-joint-chiefs-staff-cuban-missile-crisis.
3. Stern, "The Inside Story of the Cuban Missile Crisis."
4. Natalie Kitroeff, "A Prominent Mexican TV Anchor Departs. Will Dispassionate Coverage Go With Her?" *New York Times*, January 8, 2023, https://www .nytimes.com/2023/01/08/world/americas/denise-maerker-televisa.html.
5. Joseph P. Simmons and Leif D. Nelson, "Intuitive Confidence: Choosing Between Intuitive and Nonintuitive Alternatives," *Journal of Experimental Psychology* 135, no. 3 (2006): 409–428, https://www.researchgate.net/profile /Joseph-Simmons-2/publication/6940116_Intuitive_Confidence_Choosing _Between_Intuitive_and_Nonintuitive_Alternatives/links/09e4150f5ccd 8277bd000000/Intuitive-Confidence-Choosing-Between-Intuitive-and -Nonintuitive-Alternatives.pdf.

Chapter Four

1. Eric Bonabeau, "Don't Trust Your Gut," *Harvard Business Review*, May 2023, https://hbr.org/2003/05/dont-trust-your-gut.
2. Leigh Buchanan and Andrew O'Connell, "A Brief History of Decision Making," *Harvard Business Review*, January 2006, http://samuellearning.org/decisionmaking /handout1.pdf.
3. Amitai Etzioni, "Humble Decision Making," *Harvard Business Review on Decision Making* (Boston: Harvard Business School Press, 2001), 45–57, https:// papers.ssrn.com/sol3/papers.cfm?abstract_id=2157020.
4. Etzioni, "Humble Decision Making."
5. Barnaby J. Feder, "Quaker Chief, Tied to Losses from Snapple, to Step Down," *New York Times*, April 24, 1997, https://www.nytimes.com/1997/04/24 /business/quaker-chief-tied-to-losses-from-snapple-to-step-down.html.
6. Tori Fitzgerald, "Due Diligence Lessons From AOL, Quaker Oats, News Corp. and Sprint," Gryphon Strategies, https://gryphon-strategies.com/due-diligence -lessons-from-aol-quaker-oats-news-corp-and-sprint/.
7. Adam L. Penenberg, "Snapple Challenged in Wide Market," *New York Times*, July 10, 1994, https://www.nytimes.com/1994/07/10/nyregion/snapple -challenged-in-wide-market.html.
8. Neil Steinberg, "Snappled! A Case Study in Cluelessness: How One Deal Brought Quaker Oats to Its Knees," *Chicago Reader*, May 29, 1997, https:// chicagoreader.com/news-politics/snappled/.

9. Martha M. Hamilton, "Snapple Debacle Takes Toll: Quaker Oats to Replace CEO," *Washington Post*, April 24, 1997, https://www.washingtonpost.com /archive/business/1997/04/24/snapple-debacle-takes-toll-quaker-oats-to-replace -ceo/0f364664-047f-42e5-8b22-799bd285059a/.

10. Olivier Sibony, "The Business Case Against Gut Decisions," *Marker*, July 17, 2020, https://marker.medium.com/the-business-case-against-gut-decisions -2c163bab79b9.

11. "Curiosity Killed the Cat," *Washington Post*, March 4, 1916, https://en -academic.com/dic.nsf/enwiki/652042.

12. Jonathan B. Evans, *Leader Curiosity and Team Intellectual Stimulation* (Tucson, AZ: University of Arizona, 2020), https://repository.arizona.edu/handle/10150 /641700.

13. Todd B. Kashdan and Paul J. Silvia, "Curiosity and Interest: The Benefits of Thriving on Novelty and Challenge," *Handbook of Positive Psychology* (New York: Oxford University Press, 2009), https://www.researchgate.net/publication /232709031_Curiosity_and_Interest_The_Benefits_of_Thriving_on_Novelty _and_Challenge.

14. Michael Bungay Stanier, "Curiosity Is a Leadership Superpower," Duke Corporate Education, September 2020, https://www.dukece.com/insights /curiosity-is-a-leadership-superpower/.

15. Mo Costandi, "Intelligent People Take Longer to Solve Hard Problems," Big Think, June 22, 2023, https://bigthink.com/neuropsych/intelligent-people -slower-solve-hard-problems/.

16. Michael Schirner et al., "Learning How Network Structure Shapes Decision-Making for Bio-Inspired Computing," *Nature Communications* 14, art. 2963 (May 23, 2023), https://www.nature.com/articles/s41467-023-38626-y.

17. Michael Strahan, "Damar Hamlin Speaks Out on His 'Remarkable' Recovery," *Good Morning America*, YouTube video, February 13, 2023, https://www .youtube.com/watch?v=4qoLYdZOLHY.

18. Ashley Abramson, "Cultivating Empathy," American Psychological Association, November 1, 2021, https://www.apa.org/monitor/2021/11/feature-cultivating -empathy.

Chapter Five

1. Jenny Heyes, "The Human Library—'Don't Judge a Book By Its Cover,'" Napthens Solicitors, November 1, 2022, https://www.napthens.co.uk/news /the-human-library-dont-judge-a-book-by-its-cover/.

2. "Study Finds That Genes Play a Role in Empathy," University of Cambridge, https://www.cam.ac.uk/research/news/study-finds-that-genes-play-a-role -in-empathy.

3. Abramson, "Cultivating Empathy."
4. Tara Van Bommel, "The Power of Empathy in Times of Crisis and Beyond," Catalyst, 2021, https://www.catalyst.org/reports/empathy-work-strategy-crisis.
5. Tracy Brower, "Empathy is the Most Important Leadership Skill According to Research," *Forbes*, September 19, 2021, https://www.forbes.com/sites/tracybrower /2021/09/19/empathy-is-the-most-important-leadership-skill-according-to -research.
6. Abramson, "Cultivating Empathy."
7. Kara Swisher and Scott Galloway, "UFOs, The State of Tech, and Lakshmi Rengarajan," February 14, 2023, in *Pivot*, podcast, Vox Media, Inc., https:// podcasts.apple.com/us/podcast/ufos-the-state-of-tech-and-guest-lakshmi -rengarajan/id1073226719?i=1000599536709.
8. Mark C. Perna, "Why a Lack of Human Connection Is Crippling Your Work Culture," *Forbes*, October 24, 2022, https://www.forbes.com/sites/markcperna /2022/10/24/why-a-lack-of-human-connection-is-crippling-your-work-culture.
9. Mihnea Moldoveanu and Das Narayandas, "The Future of Leadership Development," *Harvard Business Review*, March–April 2019, https://hbr.org /2019/03/the-future-of-leadership-development.
10. Herminia Ibarra, "How to Do Sponsorship Right," *Harvard Business Review*, November–December 2022, https://hbr.org/2022/11/how-to-do-sponsorship -right.
11. Ibarra, "How to Do Sponsorship Right."
12. Ibarra, "How to Do Sponsorship Right."
13. Greg Lukianoff and Jonathan Haidt, *The Coddling of the American Mind* (New York: Penguin, 2019), 58.
14. "What Is Diversity, Equity, and Inclusion?" McKinsey & Company, August 17, 2022, https://www.mckinsey.com/featured-insights/mckinsey-explainers/what -is-diversity-equity-and-inclusion.
15. C. Kenneth Meyer and Lance Noe, "Diversity, Equity, and Inclusion Policies: Are Organizations Truly Committed to a Workplace Culture Shift?" *Journal of Business and Behavioral Sciences* 33, no. 2 (Fall 2021): 3, https://asbbs.org /files/2021-22/JBBS_33.2_Fall_2021.pdf.
16. Khristopher Brooks, "Why So Many Black Professionals Are Missing From the C-Suite," *CBS MoneyWatch,* December 10, 2019.
17. Rachel D. Arnett, "Uniting Through Difference: Rich Cultural-Identity Expression as a Conduit to Inclusion," *Organization Science* 34, no. 5 (September–October 2023): 1651–1996, C2–C3, https://pubsonline.informs .org/doi/10.1287/orsc.2022.1648.
18. Arnett, "Uniting Through Difference"; Brooks, "Why So Many Black Professionals Are Missing From the C-Suite."
19. Arnett, "Uniting Through Difference."

20. Te-Ping Chen, "The Horror of Realizing Everyone Can See Your Work Calendar Entries," *Wall Street Journal,* February 28, 2023, https://www.wsj.com/articles /work-calendar-privacy-49cd3378.

Chapter Seven

1. Tan Van Bui et al., "National Survey of Risk Factors for Non-Communicable Disease in Vietnam," *BMC Public Health* 16 (June 10, 2016), https://bmcpublic health.biomedcentral.com/articles/10.1186/s12889-016-3160-4.

2. Tuyet Thi Nguyen and Maurizio Trevisan, "Vietnam a Country in Transition: Health Challenges," *BMJ Nutrition, Prevention & Health* 3, no. 1 (2020): 60–66, https://www.ncbi.nlm.nih.gov/pmc/articles/PMC7664505/.

3. Hoa L. Nguyen et al., "Culturally Adaptive Storytelling Intervention Versus Didactic Intervention to Improve Hypertension Control in Vietnam—12 Month Follow Up Results: A Cluster Randomized Controlled Feasibility Trial," *PLoS ONE* 13, no. 12 (2018), https://journals.plos.org/plosone/article?id=10 .1371/journal.pone.0209912.

4. Nguyen et al., "Culturally Adaptive Storytelling Intervention."

5. Nguyen et al., "Culturally Adaptive Storytelling Intervention."

6. Claudio Feser, *When Inspiration Isn't Enough: Decoding Inspirational Leadership* (Hoboken, NJ: Wiley, 2016), chapter 3.

7. Varun Nagaraj and Jeff Frey, "Ethical Influence," *Psychology Today* blog, February 11, 2021, https://www.psychologytoday.com/us/blog/leading-in-the-real-world /202102/ethical-influence.

8. Nagaraj and Frey, "Ethical Influence."

9. Gary Burnison, *New Year, New Journey,* https://www.kornferry.com/insights /special-edition/new-year-new-journey.

10. Susan M. Jensen and Fred Luthans, "Entrepreneurs as Authentic Leaders: Impact on Employees' Attitudes," *Leadership & Organization Development Journal* 27, no. 8 (December 2006), https://www.emerald.com/insight/content /doi/10.1108/01437730610709273/full/html.

11. Cen April Yue et al., "Bridging Transformational Leadership, Transparent Communication, and Employee Openness to Change: The Mediating Role of Trust," *Public Relations Review* 45 (2019), https://www.sciencedirect.com /science/article/abs/pii/S0363811119300360.

12. Boas Shamir and Galit Eilam, "'What's Your Story?' A Life-Stories Approach to Authentic Leadership Development," *The Leadership Quarterly* 16 (2005): 395–417.

13. Valerian Derlega and Alan L. Chaikin, "Privacy and Self Disclosure in Social Relationships," *Journal of Social Issues* 33 no. 3 (1977), https://www .academia.edu/44381839/Privacy_and_Self_Disclosure_in_Social _Relationships.

14. Matt Gavin, "Authentic Leadership: What It Is & Why It's Important," Harvard Business School Online blog, December 10, 2019, https://online.hbs.edu/blog/post/authentic-leadership.
15. Shamir and Eilam, "'What's Your Story?'"
16. Shamir and Eilam, "'What's Your Story?'"
17. Shamir and Eilam, "'What's Your Story?'"
18. *Future Forum Pulse Summer Snapshot*, Slack, July 2022, p. 9, https://futureforum.com/wp-content/uploads/2022/07/Future-Forum-Pulse-Report-Summer-2022.pdf.
19. Email to Graza customers from CEO Andrew Benin, https://s.wsj.net/public/resources/documents/GrazaApologyEmail.pdf.
20. Ben Cohen, "What Happened When the Olive-Oil Startup Apologized," *Wall Street Journal*, January 12, 2023, https://www.wsj.com/articles/sorry-graza-olive-oil-apology-11673476845.
21. W. A. Hensel and T. L. Rasco, "Storytelling as a Method for Teaching Values and Attitudes," *Academic Medicine* 68, no. 8 (August 2022): 500–504, https://journals.lww.com/academicmedicine/abstract/1992/08000/storytelling_as_a_method_for_teaching_values_and.3.aspx.
22. Hensel and Rasco, "Storytelling as a Method for Teaching Values and Attitudes."
23. Hensel and Rasco, "Storytelling as a Method for Teaching Values and Attitudes."

Chapter Eight

1. Lindsay Ellis, "Your Co-Workers Are Less Ambitious; Bosses Adjust to the New Order," *Wall Street Journal*, December 31, 2022, https://www.wsj.com/articles/your-coworkers-are-less-ambitious-bosses-adjust-to-the-new-order-11672441067.
2. Shane McFeely and Ben Wigert, "This Fixable Problem Costs U.S. Businesses $1 Trillion," Gallup Workplace, March 13, 2019, https://www.gallup.com/workplace/247391/fixable-problem-costs-businesses-trillion.aspx.
3. "Hours of training per employee by company size U.S. 2017–2022," Statista Research Department, https://www.statista.com/statistics/795813/hours-of-training-per-employee-by-company-size-us/.
4. Marc Holliday, "10 Benefits of Employee Retention for Business," Oracle Netsuite, February 22, 2021, https://www.netsuite.com/portal/resource/articles/human-resources/employee-retention-benefits.shtml.
5. Holliday, "10 Benefits of Employee Retention."
6. "11 Benefits of Employee Retention," Indeed, updated February 3, 2023, https://www.indeed.com/career-advice/career-development/benefits-of-employee-retention.

7. Paul Ingram and Yoonjin Choi, "What Does Your Company Really Stand For?" *Harvard Business Review*, November–December 2022, https://hbr.org/2022/11 /what-does-your-company-really-stand-for.

8. Ranjay Gulati, "To See the Way Forward, Look Back," *Harvard Business Review*, November–December 2022, https://hbr.org/2022/11/to-see-the-way -forward-look-back.

9. Paul Merrill, "The Cautionary and Inspirational Story of How LEGO Rebuilt Itself," *CEO Magazine*, June 15, 2022, https://www.theceomagazine.com /business/company-profile/rebuilding-lego/.

10. Merrill, "The Cautionary and Inspirational Story of How LEGO Rebuilt Itself."

11. Rebecca Knight, "Is Your Team Solving Problems, or Just Identifying Them?" *Harvard Business Review*, April 14, 2021, https://hbr.org/2021/04/is-your-team -solving-problems-or-just-identifying-them.

12. Michael Lewis, "Don't Be Good—Be Great," May 2020, in *Against the Rules with Michael Lewis*, podcast, Pushkin Industries, https://open.spotify.com/episode /5VpZTdWffOIaqRbYalggtn?si=xWlJDtKrTwarcyGoLAwY3A&nd=1.

Chapter Nine

1. Garrett Wymer, "Studies Show Employers Lose Billions in Productivity During March Madness," WKYT, March 16, 2023, https://www.wymt.com/2023/03 /16/studies-show-employers-lose-billions-productivity-during-march-madness/.

2. "Vikings Clinch NFC North Title with Biggest Comeback in NFL History," NFL.com, December 17, 2022, https://www.nfl.com/news/vikings-clinch-nfc -north-title-with-biggest-comeback-in-nfl-history.

3. Archy O. de Berker et al., "Computations of Uncertainty Mediate Acute Stress Responses in Humans," *Nature Communications* 7, art. no. 10996 (2016), https://www.nature.com/articles/ncomms10996.

4. De Berker et al., "Computations of Uncertainty Mediate Acute Stress Responses in Humans."

Chapter Ten

1. See Carol S. Dweck, *Mindset: The New Psychology of Success* (New York: Random House, 2007).

2. Lydia Polgreen, "What My Father's Death Taught Me About Living," *New York Times*, October 26, 2022, https://www.nytimes.com/2022/10/26/opinion /grief-death-lessons-on-living.html.

3. Polgreen, "What My Father's Death Taught Me About Living."

4. Lucas M. Bietti et al., "Storytelling as Adaptive Collective Sensemaking," *Topics in Cognitive Science* 11, no. 4 (October 2019): 710–32, https://onlinelibrary .wiley.com/doi/10.1111/tops.12358.

5. Ken Baskin, "Storied Spaces: The Human Equivalent of Complex Adaptive Systems," *Emergence: Complexity & Organization* 10, no. 2 (January 2008), https://www.researchgate.net/publication/252553799_Storied_Spaces _The_Human_Equivalent_of_Complex_Adaptive_Systems.

6. Quispe López, "4 Signs You Have 'Main Character Syndrome,' According to Therapists," *Insider*, December 11, 2021, https://www.insider.com/4-signs-you -have-main-character-syndrome-like-carrie-bradshaw-2021-12.

7. Emily Wilcox, "Why You May Need a Healthy Dose of 'Main Character Syndrome,'" *Mind Café*, December 10, 2020, https://medium.com/mind-cafe /why-you-may-need-a-healthy-dose-of-main-character-syndrome-288ec2b34411.

8. Kashmira Gander, "Do You Have Main Character Syndrome?" *Newsweek*, May 6, 2021, https://www.newsweek.com/do-you-have-main-character-syndrome -1589245.

9. López, "4 Signs You Have 'Main Character Syndrome,' According to Therapists."

10. Elena Lytkina Botelho et al., "Research: When Getting Fired Is Good for Your Career," *Harvard Business Review*, October 31, 2018, https://hbr.org/2018/10 /research-when-getting-fired-is-good-for-your-career.

11. Callum Borchers, "Liz Truss Isn't Alone—Plenty of Leaders Flame Out. Here's How Some Come Back," *Wall Street Journal*, updated October, 21, 2022, https://www.wsj.com/articles/liz-truss-isnt-alone-plenty-of-leaders-flame-out -heres-how-some-come-back-11666361377.

12. Lytkina Botelho et al., "Research: When Getting Fired Is Good for Your Career."

13. Borchers, "Liz Truss Isn't Alone."

14. Kenneth P. De Meuse, "Learning Agility: Its Evolution as a Psychological Construct and Its Empirical Relationship to Leader Success," *Consulting Psychology Journal* 69, no. 4 (2017): 267–295, http://dx.doi.org/10.1037/cpb0000100.

15. De Meuse, "Learning Agility."

16. Daniel Victor and Kenneth Chang, "Starship Exploded, but SpaceX Had Reason to Pop Champagne Anyway," *New York Times*, April 20, 2023, https:// www.nytimes.com/2023/04/20/science/rapid-unscheduled-disassembly -starship-rocket.html.

17. Michael Roston, "Highlights from SpaceX's Explosive Starship Rocket Test Launch," *New York Times*, April 20, 2023, updated September 11, 2023, https:// www.nytimes.com/live/2023/04/20/science/spacex-launch-starship -rocket.

18. Jackie Wattles, "Elon Musk says SpaceX's Mars Rocket Will Be Cheaper Than He Once Thought. Here's Why," CNN Business, September 29, 2019, https:// www.cnn.com/2019/09/29/business/elon-musk-spacex-mars-starship-cost /index.html.

19. Elon Musk (@elonmusk), "Congrats @SpaceX team on an exciting test launch of Starship!" Twitter (X), April 20, 2023, 9:00 a.m., https://twitter.com/elonmusk /status/1649050306943266819?s=20.

20. Tim Higgins, "In 24 Hours, Elon Musk Reignited His Reputation for Risk," *Wall Street Journal*, April 22, 2023, https://www.wsj.com/articles/in-24-hours -elon-musk-reignited-his-reputation-for-risk-711f29b8.

21. Anand Mahindra (@anandmahindra), "But when you set up each initiative as a learning experiment . . ." Twitter (X), April 21, 2023, 6:52 a.m., https://twitter. com/anandmahindra/status/1649380517660459011.

Chapter Eleven

1. "Resilience," *Topics in Psychology*, American Psychological Association, https:// www.apa.org/topics/resilience.

2. Sheryl Sandberg and Adam Grant, *Option B: Facing Adversity, Building Resilience, and Finding Joy* (London: Random House UK, 2019).

3. Benjamin Hardy, *Be Your Future Self Now: The Science of Intentional Transformation* (New York: Hay House Business, 2022).

4. "Steelers Lineman Steve McLendon Mastering Ballet to Prevent Injuries," *Atlanta Black Star*, July 31, 2013, https://atlantablackstar.com/2013/07/31 /steve-mclendon-ballet-dancing-prevent-injuries.

5. Bill Joiner, "Developing Agile Leaders," *Industrial and Commercial Training*, February 2007, https://www.researchgate.net/publication/242157752 _Developing_agile_leaders.

6. Joiner, "Developing Agile Leaders."

7. Forbes Coaches Council, "13 Ways to Become an Agile Leader in Today's Fast-Paced World," *Forbes*, June 23, 2017, https://www.forbes.com/sites /forbescoachescouncil/2017/06/23/13-ways-to-become-an-agile-leader-in -todays-fast-paced-world/.

INDEX

agility, 190–192
Alder, Shannon, 197
Arnett, Rachel, 76–78
artificial intelligence (AI), 4–7
attitudes, teaching, 119–121
audience, considering, 93–96
authenticity
  emotion and, 98
  influence and, 108–109,
    110–115
  leadership, authentic, 110
  sponsorship and, 71
automation, 7–11

Backyard Hockey game
  (Humongous Entertainment),
  52–53
Barnard, Chester, 46
Baruch, Bernard, 17, 35
baseball analytics, 183–187
beginnings, forgotten, 188–189
belonging, 39, 74–78
Benin, Andres, 116–118
Blackie the cat, 49–50
Blanco, Lauren, 131–133

Bryant, Kobe, 198
Burnison, Gary, 3, 107–108

calendars, 80
Catholic Church, x–xi
Chang Can Dunk (movie), 194–195
change rapid, 11–15
characters, identifiable, 98
ChatGPT, 5–6
Chopra, Deepak, 1
Christiansen, Ole Kirk, 129
closeness, 77
Cohen, Ben, 118
Cohn, Jeff, 170
connection, human, 69–70
Cousins, Kirk, 146–147
COVID-19 pandemic, 135–136
creativity, inspiring, 130–133
creeping normality, 188
crisis, preparing for, 134–136
Cuban Missile Crisis, 35–38, 46,
  198
cultural-background stories, 76–77
curiosity, 49–51
customers, challenging, 122

daily planner example, 89–92,
100–101
Day Designer planner, 90–91
decision-making
better, 39
curiosity and, 49–51
Humongous Entertainment,
51–53
if you fear the answer, ask the
question (strategy #1), 54–56
invention of, 46–47
Office Space "Jump to
Conclusions" mat, 45–46
press pause (strategy #2), 56–59
Quaker Oats and Snapple, 47–49
start second-guessing yourself
(strategy #3), 59–62
Dell, 110–113
details, specific, 99
developmental relationships, 70–72
dimensionalization, 73
Dimon, Jamie, 32
disclosure reciprocity (Story Begets
Story), 80–81, 109
diversity, equity, and inclusion
(DEI), 74
DVD debacle, 172–174
Dweck, Carol, 160

emotion, authentic, 98
empathy
about, 67–68
ask questions that add dimension
(strategy #4), 73–74
"Cool Mom" and judging a book
by its cover, 63–67, 81–82
create space (strategy #5), 79–81

human connection and, 69–70
inclusion and belonging, 74–78
leadership development
relationships and, 70–72
Enchanted (movie), 165
engagement, inspiring, 126–128
English, Whitney, 100–101
Epley, Nicholas, 9
Etzioni, Amitai, 47
Evans, Jonathan, 50
evolution, human, ix–xi, 14–15
explosion, in story structure, 98

failure
fear of, 169–176
listing times it felt like you failed,
171–176
Musks's SpaceX, 176–178
Feit, Candace, 163
"Fern and the Bamboo, The,"
179–181
Fitzgerald, Billy, 138–141
fixed mindset, 159–160
Frank, 26–27
Frank, Beatrice, 56–57
Frey, Jeff, 106–107
"frictionless" economy, 9
Functions of an Executive, The
(Barnard), 46
funeral procession, 199–201

Godard, Jean-Luc, 45
Goodrich, Richelle E., 159
Grant, Adam, 58, 182
Graza olive oil, 116–118
growth mindset, 159–160
Gulati, Ranjay, 129

Hamlin, Damar, 59–61
Harari, Yuval Noah, ix–x
Hardy, Benjamin, 187
Heyes, Jenny, 65
history, corporate, 129–130
Hodges, Sara, 60–61
Holmes, Elizabeth, 26
human connection, 8–11
Humongous Entertainment, 51–53
hypertension in Vietnam, 103–105

Ibarra, Herminia, 71
inclusion, 74–78
influence
    anticipate the crises they might
        face (strategy #2), 122–123
    authenticity and, 108–109,
        110–115
    Coach Fitz, 138–141
    Dell reorganization, 110–113
    develop a discipline of revisiting
        your life stories (strategy #1),
        113–115
    Graza olive oil, 116–118
    "influencer culture," 106
    look back to get ahead (strategy
        #3), 129–130
    medical education, 119–121
    noncommunicable diseases in
        Vietnam, 103–105
    persuasion, manipulation, and
        coercion, 106–107
    tell the stories of how great they
        are to inspire self-confidence
        (strategy #5), 137–141
    tell the stories of problems solved
        (strategy #4), 137

transparency and, 108–109,
    116–118
trust and, 107
ultimate equation for, 107–110
inspirational leadership
    becoming an inspirational leader,
        125
    for creativity, 130–133
    for engagement, 126–130
    LEGO, 129–130
    Markham & Fitz, 131–133
    for the masses, 141–142
    for problem-solving, 134–137
    for self-confidence, 137–141
intelligence and slowing down, 58–59
intuition, lure of, 42–44

Javice, Charlie, 26–27, 32
Jobs, Steve, 19
job satisfaction, 108, 116, 127
Jordan, Michael, 181–182
JPMorgan Chase, 26–27, 32
judging a book by its cover, 64–67
judgment, questions implying,
    73–74
"Jump to Conclusions" mat (*Office
    Space*), 45–46

Karson, Michael, 166
Kennedy, John F., 35–38, 46, 198
Knudstorp, Jørgen Vig, 129–130
Korn Ferry, 3, 107–108

LawnSaber survey (fictitious
    company), 155–157
leadership development
    crises, anticipating, 122–123

leadership development (*cont'd*)
  empathy and, 70–72
  life-stories approach, 114
learning potential, 77
legacy, 198–201
LEGO, 129–130
LeMay, General Curtis, 37–38
Lewis, Michael, 137–141
life stories, 113–115
Litherland, Janet, 85
Little Mermaid, The (Broadway
  show), 161–163

Maerker, Denise, 40–42, 50
Main Character Energy, 165–166
manias and truths
  about, 3–4
  artificial intelligence, 4–7
  automation, 7–11
  managing the mania, 15–17
  rapid change, 11–15
  Tulipmania, 1–3, 16
Markham & Fitz, 131–133
Marti, Mollie, 103
Mauger, Paul, 85–88, 141–142
McCulloch, Topher, 19–20
McLendon, Steve, 191
medical education, 119–121
mentor relationships, 70–72
middles of stories. *See* You're Always
  in the Middle of the Story
mindset, growth vs. fixed, 159–160
Minnesota Vikings, 146–147, 164
Miss Understood podcast, 81–82
moment, in story structure, 98–99
Morin, Amy, 150–151
"move fast," 11–15

Musk, Elon, 24–25, 176–178

Nagaraj, Varun, 106–107
National Speakers Association, 168
new normal, in story structure, 98
normal, in story structure, 97–98
normality, creeping, 188

Obama, Michelle, 63
objective, identifying, 93–96
O'Connell, Kevin, 147
office politics, 122
Office Space (film), 45–46
O'Grady, Andy, 65–66
"Old Man on the Frontier Lost
  (His) Horse, The," 192–193
optimism
  about, 181–182
  baseball analytics, 183–187
  "DVD debacle," 172–174
  failure, reframing, 169–176
  growth mindset vs. fixed mindset,
    159–160
  hope, vulnerability of, 161
  "let's See how this plays out,"
    166–169
  The Little Mermaid, 161–163
  make a list of the other times it
    felt like you failed (strategy #2),
    171–176
  middle-of-the-story perspective
    and, 155–157
  Musk's SpaceX, 176–178
  tap into Main Character Energy
    (strategy #1), 165–166
  uncertainty and, 162–164
  the unexpected and, 164

Origin Stories chocolates, 131–133

outcome, disconnecting from,
  192–193

Pan narrans (the storytelling ape), x

Patchett, Ann, 145

pause, pressing, 56–59

Pelissero, Tom, 146–147

Peoplehood, 79

permacrisis, 13–14

Perna, Mark C., 69

Peterson, Patrick, 147, 149

planner, daily, 89–92, 100–101

Polgreen, Lydia, 163

pressure, 40–42, 46

problem, clarifying, 93–96

problem-solving
  every problem is a story problem,
    xii, 27–28
  inspiring, 134–136
  stories of problems solved, 137
  story solution for every problem, 32

Pulliam, Brian, 51–53

Pullman, Philip, 125

Quaker Oats, 47–49

questions, 54–56, 73–74

quotas, 122

rapid change, 11–15

relational authenticity, 71

Rengarajan, Lakshmi, 69, 73–74

Rent, 197–198

resilience
  agility and, 190–192
  disconnect from the outcome
    (strategy #4), 192–193

the end is the middle, 193–196

how far you've come, 182–188

middle-of-the-story perspective
  and, 155–157

revisit your own storyline to find
  forgotten beginnings
  (strategy #3), 188–189

"The Fern and the Bamboo,"
  179–181

"The Old Man on the Frontier
  Lost (His) Horse," 192–193

Robbins, Tony, 67

Roose, Kevin, 5

Rosenblatt, Kate, 166

salesforce personnel change example,
  54–56

Sandberg, Sheryl, 181–182

Sax, David, 11

"Seasons of Love" (Rent), 197–198

second-guessing, 59–62

self-confidence, inspiring,
  137–141

Self-Contained Breathing Apparatus
  (SCBA), 85–88, 141

self-disclosure, 80–81, 109

Smithburg, William, 47–48

Snapple, 47–49

SoulCycle, 79

space, creating, 79–81

SpaceX, 176–178

Spears, Britney, 161

sports fans, 145–147

Stanier, Michael Bungay, 51

status perception, 77

Stories that Stick (Hall), 30, 96–97,
  106

Story Begets Story (disclosure reciprocity), 80–81, 109

story fluency, 127–128

Story Forward leadership
about, 23–24
definition of, xii
owning one's story, 30–31
story advocate role, 60–61
Three Truths of, xii, 28–32

Story Forward strategies
anticipate the crises they might face, 122–123
ask questions that add dimension, 73–74
create space, 79–81
develop a discipline of revisiting your life stories, 113–115
disconnect from the outcome, 192–193
if you fear the answer, ask the question, 54–56
look back to get ahead, 129–130
make a list of the other times it felt like you failed, 171–176
press pause, 56–59
revisit your own storyline to find forgotten beginnings, 188–189
start second-guessing yourself, 59–62
tap into Main Character Energy, 165–166
tell the stories of how great they are to inspire self-confidence, 137–141
tell the stories of problems solved, 137

Story Needs to Be Told, A (Truth 2). *See also* influence; inspirational leadership
about, 30–31, 88–89
anticipate the crises they might face (strategy #2), 122–123
crafting compelling stories, 96–99
the daily planner, 89–92, 100–101
develop a discipline of revisiting your life stories (strategy #1), 113–115
four steps to preparing the story, 93–96
look back to get ahead (strategy #3), 129–130
the Self-Containing Breathing Apparatus (SCBA), 85–88
tell the stories of how great they are to inspire self-confidence (strategy #5), 137–141
tell the stories of problems solved (strategy #4), 137

storytelling. *See also* There Is Always A Story; You're Always in the Middle of the Story
"but first, story," 19–23
dark side to, 25–27
evolution and, 14–15
human evolution and, ix–xi
Tesla and market value of a story, 24–25

Strahan, Michael, 59–60

structure, three-act, 97–98

Swan, Lynn, 190

Taylor, General Maxwell, 36–37

Televis, 40–41

"tell me about," 74

Tesla, 24–25

There Is Always a Story (Truth 1).
See also decision-making;
empathy
about, 29–30, 38–39
ask questions that add dimension
(strategy #4), 73–74
create space (strategy #5), 79–81
Cuban Missile Crisis, 35–38
if you fear the answer, ask the
question (strategy #1), 54–56
intuition, lure of, 42–44
looking for, and expecting, stories,
199–202
press pause (strategy #2), 56–59
start second-guessing yourself
(strategy #3), 59–62
Televisa's Maerker, 40–42

three-act story structure, 97–98

transparency, 108–109, 116–118

tribalism, 74–75

trust
influence and, 107, 111–112
storytelling and, 89, 109–110
transparency and, 108–110, 118

Truths, Three. *See* Story Needs to Be
Told, A; There Is Always a
Story; You're Always in the
Middle of the Story

turnover, voluntary, 126

Uchitel, Rachel, 82

Uchtdorf, Dieter F., 179

uncertainty, 150–152, 162–164

unexpected, the, 164

"Uniting Through Difference"
(Arnett), 76–78

unknown, discomfort with,
150–152

values
authenticity and, 114
direct declarations of, 109, 128
story fluency and, 128
teaching, with storytelling, 72,
119–121

Vietnam, noncommunicable diseases
in, 103–105

Walker, Herschel, 190

Welch, Suzy, 13

Winfrey, Oprah, 181–182

You're Always in the Middle of the
Story (Truth 3). *See also*
optimism; resilience
about, 31–32, 148–149
disconnect from the outcome
(strategy #4), 192–193
the end is the middle, 193–196
how far you've come, 152–154,
183–187
LawnSaber survey, optimism, and
resilience, 155–157
make a list of the other times it
felt like you failed (strategy #2),
171–176
revisit your own storyline to find
forgotten beginnings
(strategy #3), 188–189
sports fans and, 145–147

tap into Main Character Energy
   (strategy #1), 165–166
uncertainty and the unknown,
   discomfort with, 150–152,
   162–164

Zuckerberg, Mark, 11, 14

ABOUT THE AUTHOR

KINDRA HALL is the bestselling author of *Stories That Stick* and *Choose Your Story, Change Your Life*. Her books have been translated into seventeen languages. She is internationally known for her expertise, research, and keynote presentations on the power of strategic storytelling in business and in life.

She lives with her husband, son, and daughter in Manhattan, where her favorite subway is the Q, her favorite musical is *Moulin Rouge*, and her favorite time of year is not February or July.

For more information about Kindra's keynotes, courses, and books, please visit www.kindrahall.com.